NO BUTS

TWELVE INSPIRING STORIES FROM MEN WHO CHANGED THEIR VIOLENT OR ABUSIVE BEHAVIOUR

MARGARET CHIPPERFIELD

HEMBURY
BOOKS

No Buts – Twelve inspiring stories from men who changed their violent or abusive behaviour

By Margaret Chipperfield

© 2024 Margaret Chipperfield

www.nobutsthebook.com.au

Hembury Books

ABOUT THE AUTHOR

Margaret Chipperfield grew up in North Balwyn in Melbourne and obtained a teaching certificate from Burwood Teacher's College in 1964. She spent six years as a primary school teacher before embarking on a degree in social work from Monash University.

She spent the next 25 years as a social worker, including three years working in Child Protection and some 20 years managing a range of different programs such as Foster Care, Family Counselling, Men's Violence, Drug and Alcohol Counselling, Family Support, Residential Care and Financial Counselling.

In 2005, Margaret was the recipient of the Robin Clark Memorial Award for Inspirational Leadership in the Field.

Following her retirement in 2007, Margaret became a marriage celebrant and a volunteer reading tutor in a remote Northern Territory community.

Thirteen years ago, Margaret became a co-facilitator of Men's Behaviour Change Groups at Anglicare Victoria and a long-term support group for men who wanted to continue learning and growing. No Buts is based on these experiences.

Margaret currently lives in Croydon and loves spending time with her six grandchildren and one great grandchild.

For more information visit www.nobutsthebook.com.au

PREFACE

At a time when the focus of family violence is rightly being examined and questioned, *No Buts* is a highly topical book. It presents a different perspective from many others by telling the perpetrator's stories through their lived experience. Lived experience stories are being recognised as an important way to have many mental health issues addressed.

Margaret tells of the men in a program which gave them unlimited time for learning and change, a program from which some of the participants were prepared to relate their experiences of the group and their journey to change. The stories offer hope and demonstrate that with support and skilled training, men are capable of change.

The stories of the men all tell of difficult histories, of verbal, physical, sexual and emotional abuse, often highly traumatic, often combined with alcohol and substance use, mental health issues, and financial problems, as well as stories of loss and grief. One of the key aspects of the program is that rather than continuing to use these things as excuses and continue to stay in a "victim hole" the men begin to recognise and accept and then take responsibility for their behaviour. It is only then they can start the often long and difficult change process.

Group work offers a number of highly important curative factors and although, not for all, can be a powerful agent of change.

The group provides men with the opportunity to examine their lives and the myths they have learned about what it is to be a man and to gain new mindset adjustments and behavioural techniques. It also allows men to recognise and name their feelings and to build empathy and understanding for those they have hurt. This is done in the context of trust within the group and led by the facilitators.

Margaret's book also provides hope that men can take responsibility and change.

Bruce Falconer
Clinical Psychologist

INTRODUCTION

I was sitting in my office at a social work agency, absorbed as I was in a challenging budget, when I heard a man's voice at the reception desk.

"I have a problem with my violent behaviour. Can I get help here?"

He was ushered into an interview room in the old church building, where there was a space for counselling and offices for staff.

At the time, I was the manager of an agency site that provided a range of services to the community, most of which were accessed by women and children. As a manager, I did not work directly with clients. I enjoyed my role, but I missed being able to work with people like the man who had just walked into the office.

I was thrilled that someone could be so gutsy. He named it, he owned it and he recognised that he could not change his behaviour on his own. He asked for help.

This was 25 years ago, back when Our Men's Behaviour Change Program had only just started. It was a mere blip of a response to the level of violence and abuse in the community. But it was a start, and one which I supported avidly.

The 20-week program was designed to meet the standards of the peak body for family violence in Victoria, No To Violence. It was rolled out by agencies such as Anglicare Victoria, where I worked. It covered a range of pertinent topics and gave opportunities for men with various learning styles to make the most of these. They included listening, seeing, reading, writing, drawing, building empathy via role-plays – and above all talking to and learning from other men who had been responsible for similar behaviour.

One in six women in Australia are subject to emotional abuse or violence from a male partner or family member.

Twenty percent of the adult population in Australia have reported the experience of physical and/or sexual family and domestic violence since the age of 15, according to the Australian Institute of Health and Welfare. One can only imagine how many children are directly or indirectly affected. Maybe they too have been abused, maybe they have heard Mum being abused, maybe they have seen Mum being hit or raped, or seen her crying or bruised. Or maybe they bore the brunt of a mum whose parenting was less than optimal at times. Perhaps they grew up to be violent too, or with low self-esteem or a sense of worthlessness. Their life story would be reflected in some way in the adult they became.

What, I asked myself, was the story of the man who turned up at our door, and who had been affected by his behaviour?

Statistics about family violence, when backed up by frequent horrific news headlines of domestic brutality and death, have created a society united in its condemnation of violent men and caused many people to distrust men in general. Men who are never abusive or violent may feel embarrassed that some of their gender could behave in these ways, or at times feel that to be masculine is to be automatically distrusted. This must feel very unpleasant.

This book is about men – and particularly about the fact that many men can, and have, changed their behaviour.

Seventy-five per cent of suicides in Australia are by men, according to government figures. As one man in a group at Anglicare Victoria said, "Let's face it, a real man doesn't reach out for help!" Many men I have worked with have had thoughts of suicide at some time in their lives and some have attempted it. Shame, grief and worthlessness can become heavy loads to bear. Does the thought of taking one's own life – violence and abuse of oneself – come from the same place as violence towards others?

I was left wondering. Over subsequent years, much has been made of the increase in male-perpetrated violence and abuse of women and children. Media coverage has intensified, with headlines about homicide and other physical and emotional brutalities that have rightly horrified most of the population. The government has poured money into programs for affected women and children, and still this behaviour continues. Women and children continue to be killed, maimed, and in many cases, scarred for life.

More money is spent, and should be, to protect and support vulnerable women and children.

I understand the needs of these women as I understand the impact of violent, abusive behaviour.

Long before services were funded to support women and children affected by violence and abuse, I was in a de facto relationship with a man I'll refer to as John. It only took a few months for me to lose sight of who I was, a few months of being hit, punched in the eye, kicked, having a tea towel stuffed in my mouth. He isolated me from my family and friends and opportunities to make new friends. When he was angry, John would take the car, all the money in the house and the phone so that I was totally isolated in Queensland, a state in which I knew no one.

It was the emotional abuse that was the worst; his relentless erosion of my belief that I was loved and well-regarded by my family and friends. I believed much of what he said, while simultaneously knowing what a fool I had been to think he would change for me. My regard for myself deteriorated slowly until I barely knew who I was any more.

On top of that I was a single mother to three young children from my previous marriage, whom I loved dearly. I would sit quietly in the bedroom with them reading stories when danger escalated. He rarely touched them, but once he threw one child into the pool, knowing he could not swim and knowing that I would dive in and bring him out. I knew I had to leave. One day, a good day – and there were plenty of good days – I decided to have another car key cut. I kept it hidden in the house, a "just in case" key.

Two-and-a-half weeks later, after the bedroom door had been kicked down so that I could be reached for kicking purposes, I waited until John was in the shower, grabbed the hidden car key and quietly ushered the children into the car for a day away from the house. We had a good day out and returned in the late afternoon to find that he had called my parents to tell them what a dreadful person I was.

I called my family and booked the children on a flight to their father's home in Melbourne. Two days later I was alone with John while packing my goods and planning my exit. I later heard that upon arrival at the airport one of my young sons asked my friend if she could call the police next time I was hit. This son remained cross with me for years because I had not let him protect me. He was only four years old at the time.

Like many weeks in the past, the last three weeks with John were good. The good times and bad times alternated, both confusing and disorienting me. Hope had repeatedly fought with despair. But I continued with my plans to leave. Three weeks later I arrived at my parents' Melbourne home, an emotional wreck.

I felt like an empty bucket, empty of all but guilt and shame and devoid of any knowledge of who I was. This left me with the task of refilling the bucket with careful consideration, like shopping in a market with little money.

I found a small house to rent. My priority was my children, who returned to live with me a few weeks later. My next task was to complete a social work degree so I could be in a better position to help other vulnerable women.

I was so fortunate. I had immense support from my family members and friends, enabling me to rebuild my life.

Many years later, when the young man entered the building with change on his mind, I saw the start of a new movement designed to protect women and children by helping men to change their behaviour. Could it work?

My years of social work had been in quite different fields, so I knew nothing about this new program that was sprouting from the ground and would eventually flourish. I continued in my career, managing and supporting many different services and connecting with other regional services and funding bodies to ensure a collaborative approach to the work we shared. As a manager, I was not involved at the grassroots of the Men's Violence Program, as it was then named.

I eventually retired from social work and considered what I would like to do with my newfound freedom. I decided to volunteer in the now-expanded Men's Behaviour Change Program. Although I was a social worker with some twenty-five years of experience, I had much to learn about how to help men change. I was very motivated. I also needed to test my belief that change could occur and to see those changes firsthand. I worked as a volunteer for a year or two – I think you could call it an apprenticeship – and then I was offered a job co-facilitating the Men's Behaviour Change roups.

Today we have established services, and they have grown over time. Since the services' inception, women and children have become recognised as vulnerable and requiring programs that protect and support them when necessary. We heard about their needs. We empathised with the women and children and applauded the greater provision of services for them. And we still do.

But what about the men who are perpetrators? We hear about

those who get sent to prison, but what about the others who have lost families, homes and careers as well as self-respect and any chance of liking themselves again? Some move far away and remain cut off from family. Some make new relationships and continue their abusive behaviour towards yet more women and children. But there is another group, a group that is rarely heard of: the men who want to change.

What do we hear about them? Are there any headlines or good stories about men changing their behaviour, men who take responsibility for their past behaviour and recognise with shame the impact it has had, men who not only change their behaviour but who also help other men to do so, men who move from self-loathing to liking themselves again?

I attended a function during this time, where a female acquaintance who worked with women who had been abused asked me what work I was doing. On hearing that I worked with men who had been violent or abusive, she reeled a little in horror and called me a traitor. I was stunned. It was only later, after some reflection, that I came to comprehend this response.

The woman had been working with women and children in women's refuges, which had only recently been established in recognition of their suffering and need for safe housing, and undoubtedly she had witnessed much pain and trauma perpetrated by men. She no doubt neither believed men could change nor supported the notion of funding a men's program when the money could be used to further support affected women and children. Though the incident threw me at the time, it served the useful purpose of acknowledging that I had developed complete confidence that men could change if sufficiently motivated to do so. My initial shock at her reaction simply increased my motivation to prove she and others like her were wrong. However, it could certainly be argued that we had the same goals: the safety of women and children. We were just approaching it from different directions.

My journey in the family violence program finished in 2022 after ten years, of which the last three-and-a-half were spent with a group of men who had completed the twenty-week Men's Behaviour Change Program and who chose to join a follow-up group. This second program was designed to help men sustain the changes they had made and to keep growing towards greater emotional intelligence. Most of these stories have come from this group of men.

The following stories give insight into my learnings and the courage and fortitude of a sample of the past and present members of the group I worked with. They tell their stories in their own words. While this book is about men and, in many cases, their untapped potential, it in no way diminishes the suffering that men have inflicted upon women and children. It is because of this intolerable damage that this book has come to be written: to examine the root cause of the problem and seek an understanding and some solutions.

I have witnessed enormous changes in many men. I am in no position to predict whether these are permanent, although my gut instinct is to say that most of them are. However, neither they nor I can be certain of future behaviour of either these men or men who have never been violent. Some of the men are now living alone, so their changed behaviour needs to be tested in the context of an intimate relationship, or in the context of children living permanently with them.

I put this book together in the belief that more men may change their behaviour if they were given a way of understanding the process, and the opportunity to put in the work. Twelve of the men have courageously shared their stories to motivate and encourage others, as well as to demonstrate to the world that changes can be made.

The men have written these stories, or I have written them after interviews and discussions. My drafts were corrected and modified by the men themselves to ensure their stories are authentic. Their names and other identifying details have been changed, but their truth has not.

Each man, if asked, "Who made the choice to behave with violence or abuse?" would respond, "I did". This is a huge advance on their thoughts from the day most of them started their first group. "I did" – with no buts – was the answer we were seeking.

1

THE MEN'S BEHAVIOUR CHANGE PROGRAM

I was quite nervous about my performance when I started this work. I would timidly greet the men as they entered the meeting room ahead of a Men's Behaviour Change Program. It took a while for me to remember names, as I guess it did for some of the men too. I wondered if the men were looking at me thinking, "What is that old woman doing here?" Maybe they were, given that I was fast approaching 70 at the time. But I knew why I was there. I wanted to contribute to social change, even if it were on a small level in comparison to the scale of the issue.

The groups consist of up to sixteen men with two facilitators, usually one male and one female. They are designed to run for twenty weeks. Each man is interviewed and assessed beforehand for his suitability to join a group.

I was often asked if I was scared of the men who attended these groups. Not at all. I started working with two terrific co-facilitators, one of whom had worked in the field for many years. I learned so much from them both, and it never occurred to me to be frightened of potential violence. Only twice did men speak in an aggressive way to me. One was red-faced with fury and looked as if he would explode at any minute. He contained himself. Most men were very well-mannered and respectful, reducing foul language to a minimum and behaving appropriately in the group situation.

Over the next few weeks I found myself wondering what had become of the man I had heard years ago at reception. Had he stayed the course? Had he been able to change his violent behaviour? How were his partner and his children, and where were they? Many people believe the adage "a leopard can't change its spots", but while men are not leopards and are quite capable of change like we all are, I was uncertain about whether such a transformation could occur. Surely learned behaviour could be unlearned? I would soon find out.

Some men walk into their first Men's Behaviour Change Program meeting meekly; uncertain, embarrassed and decidedly uncomfortable. They sit as unobtrusively as possible with a degree of fear of the other possibly "violent" men. Others stride in with feigned confidence and bonhomie, shaking hands and leaning forward in their chair. Some saunter in with macho arrogance, dressed in short shorts and sitting with groin and chest thrust forward. Others walk in unsure, but are polite and amenable as they seat themselves and nod perfunctorily to other men. Men of all ages and nationalities may be represented in these groups. There are tradies, technicians and managers. They come from all walks of life.

Those who come voluntarily mostly do so because they genuinely want to change their violent, abusive behaviours. They are ashamed and they recognise that this is a critical opportunity, to be grasped with both hands. Some men come voluntarily, to please their partners or to keep their behaviour away from the eyes of the law. Of those that come because they have been mandated by the court, some believe this is the best thing for them to do and are eager to make changes, while others resent the obligation to attend but consider the alternative, which is usually a jail sentence, to be far worse. Some are angry that this has been forced upon them. They think, "She made me do it", or "The system is fucked", or "I am the victim here". These are three common beliefs.

After introductions, which are often marked by the men's significant indifference towards each other, frequently based in fear, the facilitators explain a little about the group and how it will be conducted. Group guidelines are discussed and emphasised. The two most pertinent are: "Do not speak disrespectfully about any other person, particularly your partner or ex-partner, as they are not present to speak for themselves", and "Confidentiality is absolute except when limited by a duty of care". Facilitators will only share information if they consider someone may be at risk, be it a family member or the men themselves.

The first activity is exploring the definition of family violence. The course is based on this definition, which is far broader nowadays than it was when it was first recognised only as physical abuse. This used to cover a range of actions, from kicking, pushing and hitting a partner, children or a pet to the use of a weapon to murder. Much was left out.

The current definition from the peak body in Victoria, No to Violence, is as follows:

- *Family and domestic violence is any violent, threatening, coercive or controlling behaviour that occurs in current or past family, domestic or intimate relationships.*
- *Intimate partners, family members and non-family carers can perpetrate violence against people they are caring for. Young people can also use violence or be victims of violence within their family.*

The Family Violence Protection Act 2008 recognises these definitions of family violence, confirming that:

- *Family violence is a fundamental violation of human rights and is unacceptable in any form.*
- *Family violence may involve overt or subtle exploitation of power imbalances and may consist of isolated incidents or patterns of abuse over a period of time.*
- *Under the Act, examples of behaviour that may constitute family violence include (but are not limited to):*

- *an assault*
- *a sexual assault or other sexually abusive behaviour*
- *stalking*
- *repeated derogatory taunts*
- *intentionally damaging or destroying property*
- *intentionally causing death or injury to an animal*
- *unreasonably denying the family member the financial autonomy that he or she would otherwise have had*
- *unreasonably withholding financial support needed to meet the reasonable living expenses of the family member, or his or her child, at a time when the family member is entirely or predominantly dependent on the person for financial support*
- *preventing the family member from making or keeping connections with his or her family, friends or culture*
- *unlawfully depriving the family member, or any member of the family member's family, or his or her liberty.*

Online abuse was not common at the time the laws were written, but it has become recognised as a source of significant harm. Sometimes it is given as the reason for suicide. Coercive control is when someone repeatedly hurts, scares or isolates another person to control them. It can escalate as the addiction to control becomes harder to contain, and has been included more recently as a crime. It poses serious, life-threatening risks.

Every single type of violence or abuse is accompanied by emotional abuse, intentionally or not. It too leaves deep scars. The trauma associated with the abuse lasts for months, years, or a lifetime. Frequently this scarring affects the next generation and possibly the next. The men are generally shocked when this definition of violence is revealed to them, as some of their stories will show.

Most men stay in the group and connections are gradually made as the men tell their stories and recognise themselves in the tales of others. The twenty weeks of the Men's Behaviour Change Program are packed full of relevant educational material, mostly related to raising awareness and the resulting increased capacity to use some of the strategies designed to take control of their anger.

There is the opportunity for men to present a challenge they came up against during the past week. This is usually some form of abuse they perpetrated or a trigger they reacted to, or even a situation they handled in a new and constructive way. Feedback is given and thoughts are shared in a way that promotes learning for everyone present. It takes time for men to trust enough to share these sorts of experiences, especially when shame is involved. Some never do, but in many cases the men learn as much or more from each other than they do from the facilitators.

I would often see slight shifts in the thinking of the men who came in unwilling to take any responsibility for their behaviour. Sometimes a few weeks later they would be able to understand what their actions had meant to those around them.

I remember one man who was in total denial for weeks. He came in one day in an elevated mood, as if he had just found treasure. And he had. He said he had experienced, and I use his word, an "epiphany" on Saturday morning when it dawned on him that despite spending his life determined not to turn out like his violent father, he had done exactly that. It was a moment of mixed emotions; grief over the lack of a father figure whose role modelling was positive, to joy that he had recognised himself so clearly at last and could subsequently work on breaking the trans-generational link and create a positive role model for future generations. His children were about to benefit greatly. Hopefully they would learn to trust again and, importantly, he would learn to trust himself.

The men are usually uncertain about what they will gain, if anything, from the Men's Behaviour Change Program. Some think that they will leave with a bag of tools, strategies and techniques which will solve their problems if used properly. To some extent this is true, but the option of exploring one's life story and learning from past behaviour is far more likely to produce sustained change because it enables them to identify unhelpful baggage and reduce its negative impact. This is far more effective if worked through over months or even years.

Metaphorically speaking, I had to fill an empty bucket with carefully selected items during my life. The men have to examine what is already in their bucket and reconsider the value of each item. It is at times an extremely painful job, but the outcomes make it worthwhile.

We all have stories, and we are all products of those tales, at least our version of them. Given that they depend on many things such as memory, genetics, photos, physical and psychological scars as well as what people tell us, our stories are rarely accurate or comprehensive. But they are our reality, from which we emerge for better or for worse. It can be obvious that our memory is flawed when we visit the house we grew up in only to find that the actual dimensions of it do not fit the picture we have carried in our mind for so long. But whatever we felt in that house is our reality to keep or discard as we wish.

The voluntary group that follows the Men's Behaviour Change Program is a greater opportunity for men to explore their childhood and adult years. Here, there is more time to examine their own lives, learn what is meant by emotional intelligence, and add a new chapter to their story. This chapter could finish with self-respect and the safety of women, children and other men, as well as themselves, a story that may result in them liking themselves again – or perhaps for the first time.

In this second, ongoing group, which gave birth to most of the stories that follow, the course was created jointly by the facilitators and the men, according to perceived or actual need. This gave the men more control over a group whose aims they had created and whose rules they had contributed to. Such trust in the men built a sense of shared purpose and support for each other, as well as a sense of belonging.

The men agreed to write their stories because they wanted others to know that men can change. They wrote for the doubters, the disbelievers, and for all adolescents and men and women, to help them understand that violent and abusive behaviour of any kind is not acceptable and change is possible.

I asked them to write their life story. They could include any aspects of their life they thought were relevant. I also asked them to be sure to explain what sort of violence and abuse they had perpetrated, and what helped them change their behaviour. My minimal editing of the stories focused primarily on grammar and spelling. Sometimes I asked a man to add some words to better explain a point or to fill out an issue worth sharing.

Men can and do change, although there is little written evidence of this. This is not because men don't sustain the changes, but because researching such a thing is fraught and complex. However, I am told that some research is being conducted.

When we talk about the changes men make, we are really referring to exchanging harmful behaviour for helpful behaviour which ensures the safety of all and includes an increased understanding of the impact of abuse, as well as a greater level of self-awareness and emotional intelligence.

I have watched this exchange take place over time. It doesn't produce perfect men, but it can produce men who are not violent or abusive and who are far more insightful than they used to be. "I wish I had done this course years ago" is something I have heard innumerable times.

Men's openness about their participation in this group varied greatly. Some didn't care who knew, some were choosy about who they told, and some told no one. Some used the material to share with their partners or to influence friends. One man carried his file of handouts next to him on the seat of his truck so he had a permanent reminder of the changes he was working on. Their influence on men inside the group and outside it was often skillful and wise. Speaking publicly about their story of family violence was something many men were capable of, but concerns about confidentiality and the impact on their family understandably put a stop to my dreams of capitalising on their strengths in that way.

We came to enjoy the stimulation offered by relevant quotes and we would try to finish each session with one. It may have been suggested by a facilitator or one of the men. Some of us had favourites, and I have tried to head each story with a quote that seemed applicable if the man whose story it is could not find or create one. Good quotes do not necessarily come from famous learned people.

Of course, not all men make the change. This book is about those who are doing so or have done so – because it can be done.

2

JOE

"The unexamined life is not worth living."
   – Socrates

"It was a sunny afternoon in late June when my whole identity was challenged. This was the day I got served with a family violence intervention order for violence against my separated wife and children. The order stated that I was not to go near my wife or children before the subsequent court case.

It was heartbreaking to read what I had done, including accusing her of mismanaging the finances so I could control the money, complaining that our son David was just another mouth to feed now that he was born, verbally abusing her and making her friends feel too uncomfortable to visit, which isolated her as well. I had made her feel unsafe in her own home.

If I am honest, I was in shock. I had no idea I was an abusive man. I thought I knew what family violence was. It was hitting or threatening your partner or children. I had no idea there was such a thing as emotional abuse and as for financial abuse, I assumed it was when you took all of your partner's money. I had absolutely no idea I was in fact a perpetrator of family violence.

This one small interaction with the police caused me to totally change my way of thinking and acting over the last few years. I have had to look at everything I thought I knew as a person, as a father and a husband, even as a member of society in general, and I personally know this one action has improved my life.

I choose not to see the negatives of the intervention order. I choose to see and act in the positive. I have had a lot of help over the years from my original Men's Behaviour Change Program, from personal counselling, from other group change programs and from friends and family who have supported me. It has taken a lot of work from where I started, but the change is positive and permanent. Not only has it helped me and people close to me, it has also given me the tools to help friends and acquaintances with similar issues.

I can't talk about my change without bringing in my childhood and teen years. These were quite violent. It was the "typical" abusive environment we all assume when thinking about family violence.

I grew up in a very middle-class home in a nice suburb. Mum and stepdad both had well-paying jobs and we didn't need or want for anything. Grandpa lived with us so we always had someone home and this was the 1980s so we had many friends and things to do. I also had an extremely physically violent stepfather.

If I went to school with bruising or unable to walk properly it was just assumed I had done something wrong and deserved it. The neighbours, teachers, other family members, no one really said a thing. It was one of those "don't ask" things that we still do to this day if we are honest with ourselves.

As a kid I became angrier and angrier. It got to the point where the hidings stopped meaning anything. My stepdad had mental health problems and took it out on me instead of getting help, as getting help would have meant his guns were taken away. Nothing got in the way of his guns, not us kids, my mum, friends or family. Those inanimate objects ruled his life, so in the end being hit until you couldn't walk was the cost of doing business, I thought.

That's not to say I didn't have a lot of fun as a kid, I did, just not with family. I was never close to any family really. I relied on my friends to get anything positive. Unfortunately this situation continued right through my teen and adult years, until very recently.

The abuse got worse into my pre-teen years. I became angrier with everything and did more and more things wrong in my parents' eyes, things which needed to be punished. When I was kicked out of home at thirteen I thought, "Yep, I am on my way now", but I didn't realise the damage that I was carrying around with me. I buried my emotions and any feelings down deep, the deeper the better.

I now know this is what caused my explosive anger outbursts. These were almost always directed at myself. I made a couple of suicide attempts at fourteen, was in and out of foster care and then into residential homes, and finally I went to my real dad. I had never really known my biological father, as I always thought my stepdad was my father, but he did take me in when I had nowhere to go.

I went from an abusive middle-class home to an extremely dysfunctional, violent, alcoholic, low-class home. I was way out of control with everything. All through my younger years though, I never touched drugs or alcohol, I just internalised everything and totally shut down to anything and everyone.

During my mid to late teenage years I never really slowed down. After a while I ended up back home with Mum and my stepdad. Nothing changed, apart from the fact that I was really too big to be hit with a belt anymore. But there was no support as far as I was concerned.

I left school and just started working. The last straw for Mum was when Dad was going to stab her in front of us and I had to get out and call the police. The police said it was just a domestic and Dad was not even taken to the police station.

The last time Dad ever actually hit me I was sixteen. I am not sure who was more surprised, me or him, as I was not a young kid anymore and I had a lot of anger. This was the last time he ever laid a finger on me. It was not worth it for him as I could fight back.

The last time my dad and I talked he pointed a gun at me and said he would shoot me before he shot himself. We were both drunk at the time. I was scared, but my fear was tempered by anger and my belief that he didn't have the guts to shoot me. I called the police and it was the next day when the shock hit me as Dad was arrested and I realised that it was the end of our relationship. It may have been a toxic relationship, but I was still devastated. That was a lot of years ago now and we have only spoken twice on the phone since.

The first time I actually felt respect for anyone was my boss where I did my apprenticeship. This didn't stop me drinking heavily through my twenties. I also did a huge amount of party drugs and never stopped really until I met my future wife.

I started to realise there was something wrong with me internally in my late teens to twenties. I was missing something that it seemed a lot of other people had, and that was emotions. I felt nothing generally. I was not sad, angry, happy; nothing. I was just there, somewhere, totally shut down to everyone. That's not to say I was some lunatic, I managed to blend in, but I was different from most.

I did suffer quite a lot though, and did use drugs to feel anything close to normal, and I found that most people in the party scene had similar problems. We all seemed to be running from something and chasing the next good time.

I remember the day I met her, my future wife. It was a four-wheel drive trip, and I thought she was amazing. She was the first person I can remember who actually made me feel anything. I never realised the extent of my emotional damage until a lot later. I never trusted her. I don't mean if she went out. I just couldn't trust anyone with anything that could hurt me emotionally, and this was at the heart of my abuse towards my family.

In trying to keep myself safe and not wanting to explode towards my family, I shut down more – if that was even possible. I came home and literally didn't talk for years apart from "hellos" and what not. It was like living with two people inside me. I wanted so much to open up and explain what was going on inside, but I just could not do it.

That was the problem with my emotional damage, the more I avoided the more it brought it closer to the surface, and the more I pushed, the more damage I caused. I always said I am not like my dad, I don't hit my wife or kids and certainly have not tried to kill them, but I now realise how much pain I caused and harm I inflicted at an emotional level.

I avoided much of my kids' lives. The birth of my first child was a horrible experience and even now, years later, I can't see anything other than blood and can remember thinking that the baby had killed my wife. I have since learned men suffer postnatal depression as well as women, so it is little wonder I avoided being involved as much as I did.

My wife said early on that she was the mum and I could just stay out of the way. I took that literally and did nothing to help her at all. I went to work and paid the bills and that's it. I avoided so much. I never even changed a nappy.

So trying to avoid being abusive ended up a failure. I was stonewalling and living a life of ignoring my family. I never really yelled, I just shut down. When things got heated between her family and her I just said to her family, "Enough, you are not welcome here or in my kid's lives now", and that's how I functioned. I ignored everything until I **had** to get involved, then just shut everything down quickly. This had a bad effect on our marriage, to the point that my wife had to leave with our children.

When I got the intervention order, which was nearly twelve months after she walked out, and I read the allegations, I was in total shock as I had never even thought about emotional abuse and honestly at the time I thought it was a joke.

This intervention order got an emotional response from me. It nearly broke me, so I searched around for what to do as I was going to fight it all the way. I saw myself as a victim.

I found out about Men's Behaviour Change Programs. I knew I had to do something. I was in a bad place, as everything I thought I had buried came up all at once.

I drove back home from the city crying my eyes out in the truck. I had to do something. I had two options as I saw it, get into this Men's Behaviour Change Program or go to the psych ward. They were literally my only options at the time.

I went to enquire about the Men's Behaviour Change Program.

Amazingly, the lady at the counter helped me with information, and before I even walked back to my truck I was talking to the intake manager. I don't believe in God, but something happened that day.

The reason I felt I needed to get into the Men's Behaviour Change Program is because I had no idea what this abuse was all about. I needed to know why, and why I had such a response to getting the intervention order and why I could not shut down this time.

I think it took about three weeks from the moment I went into the office to actually getting a place. It was quick, very quick, so quick in fact I couldn't change my mind, and it seemed something was looking out for me again as we started night shift at work, and I was able to attend the group and still go to work. I had the most amazing work colleague at the time. She and some others helped me in a way I could never ever repay or even explain. I will never forget the support I felt.

In the group, like most men, I was very nervous going in as I suffer slightly with social anxiety. I am usually fairly quiet until I feel comfortable, but something happened, I felt comfortable. I had no trouble explaining what brought me to the group after listening to the other men, and we came from all walks of life. I won't lie and say I had a moment of clarity straight away, but I did feel I was in the right place, and I was safe, which is something I have very rarely felt in my life.

My moment came three weeks in. I was still in denial about my abuse, but as I sat there listening to another man it dawned on me that society has deemed my behaviour abusive and who was I to say society was wrong? We can't choose what parts of society we want to follow or not, and it was just like that. From that moment on I have done everything I possibly can to change and embrace the change, not for my wife or kids, for **me**.

This was all of four years ago as I type this. Since that moment on a cold miserable night my life has changed, not only through the groups but also by feeling supported to look further into my emotions and develop ways to accept what is mine, to acknowledge and not bury them deep and ruin my life any more. Through me supporting myself this change has come about. I do this for myself, not for anyone else.

Did my wife and I reconcile? No we have not, and will not. We are at different parts of our own journeys now. The marriage breakdown is not my or her fault. We just can't support each other as we both need any longer. However, we are still friends and we co-parent as well as we possibly can.

That does not mean to say I have stopped my journey of self-improvement either. I have since started a new therapy type as well, that deals with my childhood trauma, which is at the bottom of my emotional abuse history. That's not to say I blame what happened on my childhood.

The trauma I have caused is mine to carry, and to repair with my children, who have been damaged by my parenting and for whom I am currently doing all I can to support through their challenges, which are significant. I can see the cycle already repeating itself in so many ways despite every effort to change its course. It is painful to see and I feel impotent when I, despite my best efforts, cannot influence the changes needed.

However, I will keep on trying.

I would like to thank the facilitators of the various groups. Without them I don't think I would be here. I also have a closer relationship with Mum, closer than we have ever had. I have received and given a lot of support to a couple of close friends during this journey and I have an unpayable debt of gratitude for the support of a special geologist who will never know how much her support meant to me."

Margaret says …

Joe's journey was long and arduous, so one can only imagine his wife's and children's. Will the children be able to follow Joe's journey of recovery and break the cycle before the next generation appears? It is hard to recover and learn from a lifetime of emotional neglect. Joe is fully aware of the impact he has had and is desperately trying to support his children as they face their own challenges.

For Joe, it was four years of hard work before he was able to cry about his early life experiences, to free them from festering inside him and allow him the opportunity to live life unhindered by his childhood trauma. We were all very happy to hear of his final breakthrough with his counsellor. This led, after so many years, to his ability to work on experiences that had weighed him down for so long. It was inspiring to see his confidence in himself and his certainty that he will not be violent or abusive again. We felt both moved and privileged to see, for the first time since we had known him, evidence of the emotions he had kept buried.

Several other men in the group were carrying a core of grief or trauma that still remained hidden, despite other changes that had taken place. One of these men sought individual counselling at once, just as Joe had, and another wondered out loud if he might do so too and has since followed suit. The men inspired each other. Sharing experiences increased clarity and wisdom and made us collectively feel that this group was so worthwhile.

Joe felt safe on his very first night at the Men's Behaviour Change Program. I found that a few men drop out after their first night and others do so further down the track. Sometimes trust is too big an ask from the men, as is the leap towards taking responsibility for their behaviour. However, with great courage, many more men stay in the group and most eventually feel safe. This means they can share their worst without feeling judged and accept challenges without feeling disrespected or offended. Only then can they learn about themselves and how they impact on other people.

People choose to examine their story for many reasons. Curiosity and the need to comprehend was the driving force for Joe. He knew that dealing with his past would be essential to his future. Not everyone could reflect on their past life experiences, choices and behaviour. Joe's ability to do so gave others the inspiration to do this too.

So, in order to equip men to deal with the pain and shame so often associated with their earlier lives, we sought to highlight each man's strengths so that they could consciously identify what those strengths were and draw on them as needed. As Rosie Batty wisely said on the ABC television show *The Drum* on 27 May 2022, "People are more than one thing". She was talking about both men and women and it is on this premise that we strive to help rebuild men whose better sides have been subsumed by the need for control.

One exercise we put into practice was to ask each man to draw a pie chart and shade a portion in a size relevant to the amount of violence and abuse they perpetrated. This would be labelled accordingly. They would then be asked to draw at least six more pie portions of relevant sizes and write one of their strengths in each section. These were identified as the parts of them that could assist with the change process. Then we discussed how this might occur.

I was surprised at how hard this was for most men, so we helped by providing a list of possible strengths. The men found themselves identifying strengths that they could not previously have put a name to. Rosie was right. These men were not just about violence and abuse, they were a lot more than that. The "lot more" needed to be dug up, exposed to the world and put to work in the cause of change.

They were to build on their strengths without minimising the behaviour that first brought them to the group – a difficult balance to maintain. Joe did just that.

3

ROBERT

"I wonder what else I will find out that I didn't know before." – Robert

I met Robert in a café to hear his story. He seemed relaxed and comfortable about telling it. I hadn't seen him for some time. He was looking quietly confident and content, which was good to see. He shared his story calmly and clearly.

I then met both Robert and his wife, Martha, who was able to add those bits that Robert couldn't recall. As a result, his story is a fusion of information mutually agreed upon by Robert and Martha, as well as by their three children. This is a family that works together.

ROBERT WAS the first of seven brothers and two younger twin sisters. He also had two older stepbrothers. He has very fond memories of them all playing in the bushland near their home. He felt loved by both parents and part of a happy family.

That all changed when Robert was nine. He was travelling in the back of the car and his younger brother was in the front seat. His dad was driving and swerved to avoid a car coming towards them on the wrong side of the road. Their car rolled and Robert's father sustained minor injuries which were attended to in hospital. Robert was in hospital for several weeks after having glass removed from his head. The morning after the accident Robert's parents told him that his younger brother had been found dead on the road. "I broke down", Robert told me.

"Why God?" he asked. "How could this happen?"

Compounding his grief was the fact that neither he nor his dad knew just what had happened. They would talk to each other about it, but neither had any memory beyond the car swerving. Although police investigations relieved his father of any guilt, talk in the small community in which they lived made life difficult for Robert's dad. He became angry, violent and paranoid. The family moved to a small village far away. Given his dad's tendency towards mild paranoia, it was difficult to establish the true existence of community gossip, or its extent.

In the new environment, Robert's dad calmed down. But Robert found his head constantly filling with questions and an overwhelming desire to understand what had taken place. "I always wanted to find out what really happened, and I still don't know", he said. Because there were no answers, it was hard to put the matter to rest. Nightmares plagued him, and his schoolwork, which had been fine until then, deteriorated badly. "In those days people were just expected to get on with life", said Robert, who was given no extra attention at school and was moved up a class each year, regardless of the fact that he was falling further and further behind.

His parents and stepbrothers played important roles in teaching him the practical skills that would help with everyday living, so that what he lacked in school education he compensated for in life skills. He also learned some carpentry, renovating and mechanical skills.

When Robert was fifteen years old, he asked his parents if he could leave school and get a job as he was not achieving in regular education. They agreed, and before long Robert found himself milking cows for fifty dollars a week. "Even then fifty dollars was not much", he said, laughing.

The nightmares continued as Robert moved both accommodation and jobs several times, still in close contact with his family.

He met his wife while rollerskating. He was attracted to her for many reasons, but their shared love of the outdoors, camping and fishing; their interest in gardening and the environment and the fact that she was very easy to get along with were what most appealed to Robert. "She's also a very good cook", he added with a chuckle and some emphasis.

They married and had three daughters. Robert was present for all three births, which he found to be very exciting experiences. He had always loved having children around and was used to nieces and nephews playing a significant role in his life, so having children of his own was very important to him and a natural progression of the marriage he cherished.

He was especially ecstatic when, during the third daughter's birth, the doctor stepped aside and said to Robert, "You can deliver this baby". He moved into position and did just that. His face shone as he told me it was a "fantastic experience". It was no surprise to hear that Robert loved being a father and having children around the house.

Robert continued to have nightmares and his wife said he would scream in the middle of the night. She suggested he talk to someone, but at that stage Robert did not act on her suggestion. He now wishes that he had.

Robert's dad's death was a difficult time for him, and he started to drink more. Until that time his drinking had been moderate and if he drank too much he was, as Martha described it, "hilarious". Drinking was seen as "no big deal" as his family had been drinkers and no alcohol-related problems had arisen.

Not long after this, when the children were teenagers, Robert was working as a gardener in a large complex when his supervisor punched him for no apparent reason. Robert won an appeal against the supervisor and received an appropriate payout, but the incident added to his stress levels. The fact that he never understood why he was punched added more confusion to a brain that was already yearning for answers. Robert increased his drinking yet again and his behaviour when drunk started to take a different turn.

Some years later when employed in similar work, Robert hurt his shoulder and was laid off. Following surgery, he spent some time at home. Feeling inadequate and still carrying baggage from both the punching incident and the childhood car accident, Robert's drinking spiralled. He became violent and abusive when drunk.

The family got to the point where they could see the indicators of possible rage. Robert's usually blue eyes became dark, his face would close and his body would stiffen. Family members would try to divert his attention to something calming. On occasion they would hold him down. Sometimes that would work, but several times a year he would explode like a volcano, despite their best efforts. Robert would throw violent punches and scream abuse. He was out of control and dangerous.

The last time this happened Martha was home alone with Robert. He attacked her and she feared for her life. She locked the bedroom door and called an ambulance, thinking he was having a psychotic episode. Fortunately, just after Robert had broken the door down to get to her, the police let themselves in and took him into custody. He was locked in a cell overnight and Martha went to stay with a daughter. She was "quite broken up" about the whole terrifying incident.

She couldn't trust him not to repeat his behaviour, particularly if he was drinking, and so she took out a family violence intervention order against him, preventing him from seeing her. She had been very frightened and could not trust Robert again if he was drinking. She said it was altogether a dreadful experience, but it was the verbal abuse that left the biggest scar.

Once he was told the details of his behaviour, Robert could not believe what he had done. He felt terrible and although he couldn't remember much about his actions, he vowed not to touch alcohol again. And he hasn't.

Robert lived with one of his daughters for about twelve months, at the start of which he took up the suggestion that he attend a Men's

Behaviour Change Program. His daughters all found the situation very challenging. They had seen some instances of his violent behaviour and could not believe their father would behave in such a way. It was with great trepidation and after setting clear boundaries that they took him in and supported him towards recovery at the same time as supporting their mother.

Joining the Men's Behaviour Change Program turned out to be in Robert's favour. The judge recommended that he get help and Robert was able to say that he had already started working on himself. The judge scheduled a court date for two months later so he could be updated on Robert's progress and decide whether prison would be an appropriate punishment for what was serious physical and emotional abuse. Robert continued to work on himself through both group work and individual counselling with a psychologist.

It is a sad reality that post-traumatic stress disorder, PTSD, was not a diagnosis when Robert was first traumatised. By the time his crisis had been reached it was, and so appropriate help was finally available for the damage done so many years ago. The ongoing effect of alcohol on Robert if he had not been suffering from PTSD will never be known.

The judge did not jail Robert. He continued his group work, moving from Men's Behaviour Change Program to the follow-up program and he remained alcohol-free. His wife cancelled the intervention order and allowed him back into the home a year later, on the condition that he sleep in a spare room. Slowly the relationship improved. She started to trust Robert again. Today they are very good friends. He bought her a friendship ring, and her acceptance of it represents what Robert describes as "a lifelong friendship".

Robert maintains close relationships with all three of his daughters, who have also built trust in him again. They have been supportive and encouraging of his change and have said that he seems calmer, more relaxed, and more able to discuss important issues.

Robert continues to work on himself. He now recognises when he is becoming tense. "My body aches all over", he said. He has started meditating at such times until he feels calm again. He has meditation apps on his phone and can use this strategy to calm himself as necessary.

When I asked him if he liked himself, his response was "I actually have some love for myself now and I haven't had that since I was a kid".

I asked Robert what had helped most in making changes to himself, and he said firstly communication. He explained that he used to respond to anything anyone said, particularly his wife, with "Oh yeah" and a nod of his head. He told me he used to not know what to say. Now he has learned about empathy, his communication is quite different. He didn't know what empathy was, but now that he does, he can use it appropriately and it has helped to improve his relationships.

Recently, their dog had to be put down. His wife was quite distressed about the loss of the much-loved pet. Robert put his arm around her, cuddled her and affirmed that she had made the right decision as it was necessary to put the dog out of pain. He told her he understood she would miss their dog. In the past he would never have known how to respond in this way.

Now that he can respond with conscious recognition or understanding of the issue, he can also suggest possible solutions, something he would never have done before. "Perhaps you could try this", he said when his wife recently described a sticky situation at work. What new behaviour this was, and how much more caring of his wife and satisfying for Robert.

Then he volunteered, "If I'm not feeling quite right, I take a break and come back and continue the discussion later". "Time out?" I asked. "Yes", said Robert, "I learned that in group too".

Robert agreed that he had done a lot of learning that he needed to apply to his relationship with his wife, his children and the wider world, and although he was well on the way, there was more to do yet.

I asked Robert what he thought should happen to tackle the problem of violence and abuse of women and children. He immediately said, "It needs to start in the schools. Boys need to be taught to respect girls, and boys need to know that it's not just okay but important to show their feelings. My dad was never taught that, and he could never show his feelings in any way. He couldn't even give us a hug. We knew we were loved because of the many things he did for us, but a hug would have been good". Robert added that learning to recognise and show feelings might have saved him the distress of holding them back and failing to acknowledge and deal with them.

"And alcohol", he added. "The possible effects of alcohol need to be spelled out very clearly. I certainly had no idea it could affect me that way. I wonder what else I will find out that I didn't know before."

Robert's wife, Martha

Between the Robert I knew and the Robert I know today, there has been a long journey.

We met and I felt a connection. A short time later we were married. I knew that Robert had some issues in his education, but he was a very happy person. His eyes smiled a stunning blue, and still do today. His family were big party people with whom we always had a laugh. That was so different for me as we came from diverse ways of life. Mine was very strict and tough and the complete opposite of Robert's, yet both were loving families.

Along our journey we had tough times. We lost our house due to a recession and moved around for eight years from Millgrove to Ararat, to the east of Melbourne, and to this place here for the past 31 years. It took its toll and both of us started to feel the pressure. Robert's nightmares got worse. Money issues were a major problem and Robert's illiteracy left us not knowing how to acknowledge this issue. There was not a lot of help around to support him. Finding jobs became a problem and being bullied did not help. He believed drinking was a party, not a life choice. Robert got less involved in social events as he felt like people were controlling him.

He was finally diagnosed many years ago with PTSD, but did not want to accept it as it made him feel stupid. That – stupid – is something he is not, and he has realised today that it's not something I see in him either. The happier person I met has come back through this tough time, guided by counsellors, the men's group and by family members, and with the realisation that he is not the only one with stories like his. He listens more and even through challenging times he is no longer lost, sitting on his phone and ignoring the world. He now calls his daughters or talks to me and his psychology support worker.

He helps more around the house. He has been happy, without anger, for me to help with the finances. Going through the men's group was the best thing as it gave him ways of learning to listen and to trust and believe in himself more. He's happy to keep practicing what he has learned and keep doing more to better himself by accepting his losses and recognising his happiness. He meditates and he goes for a walk regularly to wake himself up and relieve stress. Robert talks to people so much more easily today, just as he did so many years ago.

My main statement is that the family loves him as the fantastic, singing, joking man he is.

The help from the psychologist and psychiatrist has always been important, but men's groups are a fantastic way to learn more. No matter whether male or female, respect is always essential, and it needs to be taught in schools by teachers who are trained to teach this sort of thing. Not all parents know how to teach respect.

A struggling child needs help to move them on. They need acknowledgment and support. In Robert's case, his family were grieving, so someone needed to step in. But it didn't happen. I understand this can be difficult, but if children understand it's okay to feel and show and talk about their feelings, how much better off the world will be.

That is how we raised our girls. Robert was the best at helping them to learn and believe in themselves. He had lost that belief in himself, and now he's back helping our girls to make changes and teaching the grandchildren that feelings are okay. I see him smiling again. I say, "Smile, be happy and have fun, and always know you are loved".

Thanks to you all for reading this and the biggest thank you to the people who supported him through this group. Please don't stop this help and support. It is needed.

From Martha

Margaret says ...

Robert learned much from listening. He spoke little in group, but this story shows how much he took in. Robert had shared the major parts of his story with the group and joined in when asked to, but otherwise he took a back seat. I guess this was explained in part in his story when he told of not knowing how to respond to things others said.

Robert never used the word "but". He simply explained the facts as they were, neither embellished nor exaggerated. Although he spoke infrequently, his calm delivery gave a strong impression of complete authenticity.

It would have been easy for him to excuse or minimise the abuse on the grounds of PTSD, and there is no doubt PTSD played a major role in understanding his behaviour. But the men were encouraged to take responsibility for their behaviour despite any experiences that may have negatively impacted their lives.

As a society we generally raise our kids as fairly as we can, but do we educate them about the fact that the world is not a fair place? That people have vastly different life experiences and that we must choose what we do with the life experiences to which we are subjected? Many men could tell similar stories to those in this book, yet they have not chosen to behave with violence or abuse. Our behaviour, no matter what the provocation or circumstances behind it, is our choice. For some, the choice is much harder than for others, but no matter how hard, the choice is still ours. Once this is recognised, change can happen.

When Robert realised what he had done to his wife, he knew he had to make a choice. He chose not to drink alcohol again. And he hasn't.

Many of us inherit goods and chattels from our parents and we choose those that we want to keep, planning where we will put them or how they will be used, and send the rest to charity. These are conscious decisions. However, we also inherit personality characteristics from our parents, some great and some not so good. Do we do the same with those, separating the wheat from the chaff? Do we make a conscious decision about whether we want a particular trait to be part of our personality? Are we selective in a carefully considered way, aware that some work may be required to support the choices we make?

It often takes a crisis to enable us to be consciously selective. Robert's crisis was his physical violence towards his wife. His shame became his motivation to change. From a dangerously violent drunk, he has become a sober, caring and happy man who has grown to love himself again and to show his love for others. From feeling frightened and unsafe, his family took a calculated risk to trust Robert again.

4

THOMAS

"I believe that although it is not your fault for what happened to you as a child, it is your responsibility for how you behave as an adult. Respond, don't react. I have learned also that this is always a work in progress." –
Thomas

"Changing my violent and abusive behaviour meant above all learning to manage my ADHD. This condition is frequently misunderstood and is thought to refer to someone who cannot sit still and concentrate. No one who knows me would consider me hyperactive at all. ADHD is a much bigger and more complex challenge than that. However, ADHD does not constitute an excuse, merely an understanding of a major challenge I needed to integrate and manage in order to become a man who neither physically nor emotionally hurt anyone else, particularly my family members.

My life started happily in country Victoria. I felt loved by my parents. I enjoyed life in a farmhouse on acreage. I had friends and was happy in my first two years at school, during which I managed the work reasonably well.

I was moved into a third grade class, which separated me from all of my friends. Acquiring friends was not easy for me, and it was early in that year when I was trying to adjust to this change in my fortunes that I was required to perform an IQ test. This test changed my life. I scored very highly, which was not appreciated by my classmates – particularly as I was seen as the new boy in class who had scored higher than those who had expected to top the class.

I became a mixture of lonely, very confused and fearful at school, despite some happy times in the outside world that provided some balance for a while. I enjoyed a choir I became part of, loving the harmonies that combined to create beautiful sound. Yoga was good for me and a church youth group provided me with the opportunity to behave like my authentic self, say what I thought, use my humour and enjoy music. I also learned to play the guitar, which became a great source of satisfaction during my life.

However, when it was discovered that I had a high IQ my relatively average achievements at school gave rise to the question why was I not doing better at school. Given that ADHD was little known at that time, my parents and teachers concluded that I was just not putting in enough effort. It was all my fault. My social life deteriorated, I was belted frequently by my father, who usually did so with out-of-control, enraged yelling. My mother and teachers also meted out corporal punishment on me.

It must have been so confusing for them. They didn't know that sometimes I was given tasks which seemed as confusing as trying to travel around Australia using a map of France.

They didn't know that some undertakings had what seemed like a "force field" around them, repelling me from becoming interested or involved.

They didn't know that at times getting up in the morning was thwarted by my inability to decide what to do first.

They didn't know that I was unable to link behaviour to consequences, so I just thought getting beaten was the way life was.

Neither did they know that I was moving to the fringes of friendship groups and that my increasing vulnerability and inability to hide it resulted in me becoming an easy target for bullying.

Nowadays, I see my high IQ as a blessing, but as a child with no understanding of my yet-undiagnosed condition it was a burden indeed.

My last two years were to be spent at a Catholic college, but I left when I was repeating Year 11. The future loomed like a vast tidal wave that I could not see my way around.

My work life varied as I moved from job to job. The quality of my work ethic and output was never in question, but my inability to complete a task within the required timelines destroyed my hopes of retention at many jobs – particularly carpentry, which I so enjoyed.

I became increasingly anxious and frustrated and sought psychiatric help for depression. Medication did not help particularly, but I kept trying to obtain and hold whatever jobs I could. My application to the armed forces brought some good news, despite being knocked back on the basis of previous contact with a psychiatrist and the need to take medication regularly. Being told that my problem-solving capacity was "off the charts" was a well-needed boost.

My partner at the time was a lovely woman, but the match was not quite right so I finished the relationship and through another friend, met Jackie. We hit it off pretty quickly, sharing a similar sense of humour and appreciation of music as well as the use of "long words", as the friend who introduced us said.

It was on and off for a while and then Jackie decided she wanted to fulfil her dream of going to teach English in Japan. I could see that this was important to her, so I supported her right through this adventure, although we were not officially a partnership during that time. After the horrific Twin Towers event in New York, Jackie felt a little scared of a world in which such a thing could happen and she packed up and returned to Melbourne.

Fortunately, Jackie returned to me and we were soon living together and ultimately married, happily, but also because it was customary to do so in those days.

Both before we were married and after, we tried to have a baby. Following a stressful time of uncertainty, poor communication and some counselling, we decided to try the in vitro fertilisation program. The day before we were due to start, Jackie discovered she was pregnant. We were delighted. The pregnancy was normal, but the birth was complex and resulted in an emergency caesarean section, leaving me standing alone in the hospital corridor wondering if my wife and baby were going to be okay. It was simply dreadful.

When everything turned out well with both Jackie and the baby I was overjoyed. The first time I held our baby I was awash with love, the likes of which I had never felt before.

Our baby girl, Susan, had trouble feeding, which understandably stressed Jackie. I was used to babies as I had helped my mother when my brother was born when I was twelve, so I enjoyed getting her to sleep. Jackie returned to work for the sake of her mental health.

A miscarriage followed. For Jackie, the grief was enormous and her way of coping was to lock the pain up. Given that I couldn't openly discuss the matter with her, I inferred that I could not talk to anyone else about my pain. I was at a loss and I struggled to handle my grief on my own. Subsequently, I have never really addressed it. In retrospect, I think this was the start of a decline in our capacity to work through painful issues together.

When the news of our third pregnancy came, we were happy, but our joy was tinged with anxiety given our past experiences.

Just before our second child was born, I was diagnosed with ADHD. I was to learn much more about it and although it manifests differently in different people, I found that many of its most common characteristics were very familiar to me.

If I am upset about something, an oversupply of impactful emotions results in overreactive behaviour.

If I take no medication, I have difficulty stringing words together.

Medication helps somewhat, but getting into a habit, a routine if you like, is particularly useful as it removes the need for decision-making and gets the tasks completed. Unfortunately, while habitual behaviour is helpful to me, it can be very hard for someone else to cope with and it is not something I can easily change – or even want to.

At this time I was also made redundant from my telecommunications job.

My self-esteem was at an all-time low, but my psychiatrist gave me hope when informing me that with a diagnosis in hand, treatment through the right medication would improve my life greatly. This was excellent news.

Treatment did help, but the "right" medication was elusive. Over a long period of time and a range of different medications prescribed by a range of different professionals, progress has been minimal and I am still searching for answers. I have a referral to a well-reputed psychiatrist, but with her waiting list, an appointment seems extremely unlikely. I don't know what to do next about this.

Our second babe was born – to our immense joy – and given that my next attempt at work failed to advance me past the probationary period we decided that I would be stay-at-home Dad and Jackie would go to work.

I was happy with this, but given my symptoms and my inability to control some of them, I was unable to be a very successful houseparent. Jackie found her frustrations increased when I didn't accomplish all the jobs that required doing around the house.

I was easily annoyed and frustrated and that frustration was ramping up as time went by. My friendships fell away, which meant I had no one to talk to or share my frustrations with. I got to the stage where I shouted at Jackie, put her down and pointed out the flaws in her arguments. I would overreact to criticism and I developed a pattern of yelling abusively at my wife, particularly if I thought I was being accused of something I didn't do. I found, and still find, perceived injustice hard to tolerate. I realise though that this does not excuse my behaviour, which also included gaslighting – by which I mean psychologically manipulative behaviour which though unintentional was very harmful.

I shudder to think what effect this had on the children, but I guess they concluded that grownups don't trust each other and I imagine they felt destabilised, unsafe and anxious.

However, it was my frustration with my daughter that led me to my lowest point.

I was trying to get Susan into the shower by pushing and shoving her while yelling loudly. I realised that my behaviour was not okay and called my wife and discussed the situation with her. She spoke to our daughter and calmed her down. We discussed the matter again over the next two days, at which stage my wife asked me to leave.

I was devastated and very sad, and confused as to how the situation had escalated to this point, but I recognised that something was wrong and since I didn't want to repeat the sort of parenting I had received from my father, I sought help.

I called the men's referral line which put me on to the Men's Behaviour Change Program. At an intake interview I was asked a list of questions that immediately raised my awareness of the breadth of men's violence and abuse, and the relevance of some of it to me. I had learned my first lesson already.

Approaching the first night of the program, I was filled with trepidation. What would these violent men think of me? What would their behaviour in the group be like? My anxiety level was high. It was reassuring to hear the group rules presented, and even more so to discover that not only did the facilitators enforce the rules respectfully, but some of the men helped to ensure the rules were upheld in an appropriate manner.

It took about three weeks for me to feel a level of comfort that equated to trust of the group, at which point I could admit my mistakes and start learning from everyone else. That was a turning point.

The first very important thing I learned was that I needed help in recognising the difference between the goals I thought I was heading for in life and the harsh reality of the path that I was on, and its similarity to that of my dad's. As a teenager, I had consciously resolved that I would treat people differently from how my father treated me. However, step by step over time, it seemed my reactions were taking me on the same path as my dad, and it wasn't until I recognised this that I was able to consciously exchange my automatic, defensive reactions for considered responses in line with my values and beliefs. Having strong feelings like frustration and anger was still acceptable, but what I did with them was behaviour I could change. And I did. Most of Dad's life was lived without a diagnosis of ADHD. I had been diagnosed with ADHD only in recent years and was taking medication for it. My awareness of this disorder greatly increased my capacity to change my life around. I now had a clearer map to guide me.

I knew by then that it could lead to immense frustration and even anger as the brain struggles to transition from one thought or activity to another. It can take time and huge effort to make such transitions that other people make daily without thought. Hence the word "slow" is frequently and perhaps accurately used, if taken literally to describe my progress through tasks. Though the intelligence is there, the speed with which that intelligence can move from one topic to another is the challenge, as well as other issues such as lack of sustained concentration and lack of understanding of consequences.

My behaviour as a child with ADHD must have been very frustrating for my parents, both of whom used corporal punishment on me, as did the school on some occasions. Dad's hitting of me with hand, ruler or belt was carried out frequently and most often with shouting and no control, and I was unable to draw a line between the punishment and my behaviour. This association remained a fundamental misunderstanding for me. The connection that was necessary to assist me to correct or direct my behaviour in another direction was just not there.

Given that both of my children have been diagnosed with ADHD I am in a good position to really comprehend some of their feelings and behaviours. I am reminded of Albert Einstein's quote, "If you judge a fish by its ability to climb a tree, it will live its whole life believing that it is stupid". I have certainly experienced that and I am determined my children will not.

Many techniques designed to appeal to men's different learning needs were employed in groups, and the one that most impacted on me was role-plays. In fact, some had a profound impact. I recall one in which the men sat on the floor as children do and the facilitators played the roles of husband and wife yelling at one another while standing way above the heads of the "children". It was great learning opportunity for all present, but hard for those who were flashed back to their childhood reality and hence, I am told, this role-play was discontinued. However, it was a terrific lesson in empathy. In the heat of the moment it is easy to forget what others may be experiencing. When it is possible to tune into their feelings, one's interaction with them or in their presence may be very different and likely helpful rather than harmful.

This particular role-play also highlighted the reactions of the children to their parents. Some felt protective towards mother, others took Dad's side, and others were simply confused and bewildered. Some cried, some withdrew, and some shouted at their parents, but all were affected.

It reminded me pointedly of the need for empathy for my wife. Understanding what she was thinking and feeling changed my responses to her to more caring and more helpful, not all the time but increasingly, and with lots of practice. I am still learning to be assertive and compassionate at the same time. It's tricky, but as co-parents we need to be able to communicate effectively and constructively in consideration of all members of the family.

I can't emphasise enough how important empathy is. I learned to flick a switch to recognise what the children were feeling and respond appropriately. It enabled me to recognise the impact of my daughter not taking her pills and it moved me from battling an adversary to working together to solve the problem at hand. That was a major shift.

Another significant shift was the ability to recognise that hurtful criticism may in fact be a reflection of the person making it. This increased my ability to depersonalise criticism and it taught me that it was possible not to take it personally. That was a key learning for me which unlocked the choices of seeing things differently.

I found the regularity of groups a particularly useful tool for keeping me on track, reminding me of the changes I am trying to make and measuring my progress towards newer, healthier goals. This weekly commitment embodied good habits and practising "best" behaviour even if it involved some discomfort.

I valued the mindfulness exercises, usually carried out at the start of group, as these tended to relax and focus me, something I need to practice more at home. I greatly appreciated listening to the challenges of others and how they deal with them. What a lot of learning there was there.

Of particular value also is the way the group constantly highlights the distinction between its members grumbling about the wrongs of the world and what others should be doing to fix it and what is wrong in our lives and what we can do to best fix those problems. The legal system is a common topic, particularly for those whose behaviour has reaped legal implications, but it is not something we can change, so we are brought back to our reality and that which we can constructively contribute to through our changed behaviour.

I recently took my children away for a few days to visit other family members. As a single parent, and despite my less than illustrious history as a father, we had a great time and encountered no unsolvable problems. I was delighted to have earned their trust back and proud of my skill at single parenting and my progress down the path of change."

Margaret says …

This story has been very much a joint effort, with Thomas and I occasionally changing seats to and from the chair in front of the laptop. I found that I learned a lot from our time writing together and I began to wish that I had heard everyone's full story when I first met them, a task that would be more time-consuming than the group process would allow.

I learned and understood so much more about ADHD from Thomas. This knowledge gave me the insight and courage to almost harass him to complete this task or meet with me again to get the job finished. Thomas seemed perfectly happy with me doing this and we struggled together to explain certain concepts in ways that were right for him.

I was impressed by Thomas's determination to understand ADHD and its impact on him, as well as how it may impact other people differently. He was able to draw on his experiences and knowledge to better understand and assist his children. Empathy became a driving force in his care of them. He was able to share with his daughter's teacher both an explanation and his understanding of the effect of ADHD on Susan's capacity to follow instructions and respond in the same way as other students.

His knowledge also enabled him to comprehend the effect of his behaviour on his wife. This didn't necessarily mean he could change all the behaviour that was hard for another person to cope with, but it certainly increased his patience, tolerance and empathy. As a result, his communication style changed and he was able to respond with calm consideration instead of reacting with excessive and unhelpful emotion, as he had been prone to doing.

Another learning that supported this was his recognition of the different ways in which criticism can be interpreted. This gave rise to his awareness that he need not take criticism personally. This truth released Thomas from the endless conflict between self-doubt and anger at perceived injustice. It brought him to the point of consciously deciding whether the criticism that came his way was saying something about him that he needed to learn from, or was saying something about the person delivering the criticism and the context in which it was delivered.

Thomas considers role-plays one of the best contributions to his learning. They certainly can be very useful, but they can be very confronting as well, as was the one he refers to. That particular role-play not only highlighted the impact of the abuse on the wife, but also the myriad of impacts on the children who are exposed to violence or abuse. Children put many interpretations on their parents' behaviour, and often these are hidden from sight. In this particular role-play the men varied in their "child" responses, which included anger at Dad for his abuse, anger at Mum for not retaliating, fear, an assumption that this behaviour was somehow the child's fault, an urge to punish Dad and protect Mum, as well as a desire to be bold and powerful like Dad. Thomas was a wise man who showed great insight into many situations and who was able to tie this role-play to the importance of empathy for his wife and children.

Three years ago Thomas was supported in group as he tried to clamber out of the victim hole, that spot where a person feels sorry for himself and blames others or minimises the damage he has done in order to avoid facing the shame. He is now out of that hole, well-grounded and able to manage his behaviour in a much more helpful way, notwithstanding levels of anxiety that pause his progress at times. He has maintained a positive relationship with his children and is co-parenting with his ex-wife in a way that is increasingly amenable to all parties. His wisdom is of great benefit to others and his progress exemplifies the quote with which he started his story.

5

———

SALVATORE

"I'm always amazed at how little I know." – Salvatore

"I was born and raised in the inner suburbs of Melbourne, Victoria, by European immigrants. My father had a hard upbringing on farmland and my mother was raised in the city. She was spoilt as the youngest in her family and privileged with university education.

I was spoilt as a child and given great birthday gifts by doting relatives and parents. As I grew older it was clear to my parents that my Australian friends weren't up to scratch. I was growing long hair, wearing denim jackets and staying out late, clearly the influence of poorly chosen friends, they thought. It didn't help that I was slacking at school. Any infractions resulted in corporal punishment. Coming home late meant my father using his belt or my mother pulling on my sideburns. This all happened out of view of my friends. My parents would go wild with rage, whacking me over my head with wooden spoons, slapping and yelling.

I was sent to a Catholic boys school where you were either a "wog" or a "skip". Soccer vs football. However, within the "wogs" there were Italians, Greeks, and "other". I was a "wog" in the "other" section, picked on by the skips and the wogs. It was lonely.

As I got older I started to fight back, retaliating against the bullies at school and standing up to my parents. This was not done in an abusive way, but by standing up straight (I am tall), puffing out my chest, holding my chin up, making direct eye contact and confidently saying that I will have none of that. I avoided my parents where possible. Now I'm over fifty and I haven't spoken to them for more than fifteen years, since before my third child was born, for reasons not only associated with their abuse of me.

I met my wife in my early twenties. She is a few years younger than me. We got married when I was thirty. We had two daughters and a son when I was aged thirty-one to thirty-six.

Marriage and children were great. It wasn't until my children started secondary school that I realised that their friends weren't "up to scratch". My children's grades were low due to their laziness and their attitudes were most frustrating. This situation was almost identical to what I experienced with my parents. I started to lash out at my children, shouting, belittling, nagging and generally behaving as my parents had done, without the physical abuse.

There was a lot of yelling in the house. It was constant. My daughters, my wife and I would all have screaming matches about boys, friends, alcohol, school grades and laziness. It was madness, and unhealthy. Sometimes we didn't care if we had guests over or if we were out in public. It got to the point where other families, friends and strangers would call us out and ask us to stop.

I treated my family like I treated my employees and colleagues. If they did not meet my high expectations then they were reprimanded or fired. By not having that control over my family and running out of options, I reverted to some of the behaviours that I had learned from my parents: belittling, yelling and humiliation. It was severe emotional abuse.

I had concerns about what I did when I become angry, or what I might do to those around me. I had been raised to be at the top of my game. Consequently I criticised how others looked and behaved. I insisted on having the last word and I forced my decisions onto others. If I didn't get my way I would sulk and storm out without discussing things. I was rude to my partner's friends. I didn't like them and they didn't like me. I played a lot of mind games and being passive–aggressive was my main weapon.

In their late teens, both my daughters attempted to take their lives. The eldest tried taking pills and the younger had a psychotic episode and expressed the desire to kill herself when confiding in her psychologist. The psychologist informed the Child Protection team in the Department of Human Services, as a duty of care. That information, when combined with the knowledge that my eldest was in hospital, resulted in a demand that I come in for an interview. The family dynamics were out of control. It was at this point that Department of Human Services (DHS) recommended that I join the Men's Behaviour Change Program.

Joining the program made a positive change in my life. The ongoing program, designed for men who had completed the Men's Behaviour Change Program and wanted to sustain the changes they had made, had a significantly greater impact. I was able now to put labels on my behaviours and that opened my eyes to a broad spectrum of feelings, thoughts and behaviours. It was akin to switching from a black-and-white television to a colour one: the same picture and motions, but with real depth and clarity.

What really helped was to first say out loud what I had done in the way of violence or abuse. Reciting it is powerful as it breaks through any denial and minimisation and moves you straight into vulnerability and shame. From there I was able to forgive myself for what I was and commence being a better man, shedding the old skin and starting anew.

While I thought I was on a journey to becoming a better man, it did not appear that way to those who knew me. No amount of trying to convince my family and friends worked. It did not help that I occasionally lapsed into my old bad behaviours. However, over time I became better at remaining in control despite being tested. New arguments or bad scenarios will frequently pop up. Job losses, Covid lockdowns and deteriorating mental health are all potential triggers of my abusive behaviour, but my control continues to improve.

The group of men that I meet with weekly are my saviours. We all have that bond and understanding about how hard it can be to remain on track. We were all in that deep, dark hole together and have great empathy for each other. That connection greatly accelerates recovery, much like making slight adjustments to the steering wheel in a fast-moving car in busy traffic.

Over time, by recognising my triggers and symptoms before the bad feelings got too strong and much earlier than racing bad thoughts took control, my behaviour improved. Over several months I paused and reflected that the home is quieter, my friends are genuinely happy to chat with me, and there is much less friction at work.

The changes occurred in several stages. It was not like a light had been switched on, but rather a gradual transition from a toxic environment where family members stayed in their rooms as much as possible, avoiding other family members, particularly myself, because of the incessant loud shouting, arguing and abuse.

The first stage which I call the "library" stage, was highlighted by the fact that people came out of their rooms and quietly mingled with each other to cook, eat, watch television and even tentatively to talk to each other and discuss their day, perhaps superficially but it was a start.

The second stage I call the "professional" stage. This was a return to noise, but of the constructive, collaborative kind. This was more relaxed and saw people sharing ideas and opinions without fear of stress or tensions arising. People felt more able to be their authentic selves.

Finally, there was a return to what I call "family life", when family members would share photos, jokes and laughter, and more intimate stories about their lives. This was the most satisfying stage of all, and the stage which made me realise what our family had been lacking for so long – a level of trust that created an atmosphere of ease and comfort.

I haven't discussed these changes with the family as I felt uncomfortable raising matters to do with past trauma, but I will seek their opinions on my writing to be sure my story is endorsed by them should it be published.

I think my wife would agree that I am willing to listen to her without argument, and even with empathy when required. I also initiate activities that we can do together, something I rarely did in the past.

I engage with my kids in a nurturing way now, rather than behaving as if they are an inconvenience. My eldest recently messaged a friend that I was her "role model", a comment that generated much sorrow at my previous failure to be the dad I should have been.

My middle child seeks me out to problem-solve and defers to me frequently in this process.

My third child seeks me out to ask if we can go bike riding together again. I can see the changes in the kids by their different behaviours with me, and this gives me great joy.

It is as though the dark aura that I had is now gone and people are less threatened by me.

I eventually showed this story to my family. I had been reluctant to as I didn't want to remind them of past trauma. They all read it and the only comment received was when one child pointed out a spelling mistake. I know my family well enough to know that if they found the story to be incorrect or offensive they would have said so. I conclude that my story is an accurate reflection of what once was and what is now."

Margaret says ...

When Salvatore first came to the second group, his behaviour had moved from openly shouting at and abusing his family to what he referred to as passive aggression. The noise level at home had abated, but much of the abuse had not, as illustrated on his first night in the group session, which will be long remembered by everybody who was there.

Salvatore presented as an intelligent, outspoken man with clear opinions he was happy to share and a good sense of humour. Before very long, he made a derogatory comment about one of his children, and he was faced with the accountability of the group. One of the men immediately informed him that we don't speak that way about our children here and Salvatore, to his enormous credit, took the words on board. He not only recognised and acknowledged their truth, but from then on he told the story to many newcomers, to the amusement and encouragement of us all.

Two men made their mark that day: the man who challenged Salvatore in an appropriate manner and Salvatore himself, who on his very first night was able to handle the confrontation in an emotionally mature way. It was an event not to be forgotten.

Salvatore turned out to be completely honest about his behaviour and a man of humility. He could acknowledge his own failures in a clear and articulate way. One is not left wondering just how he behaved; his honesty was at times disarming, but his abusive behaviour was always spelled out candidly when required. Neither is the reader left wondering about Salvatore's impact on his children. It was severe to the point of being life-threatening, not what he intended, but preventable when he chose to make changes. Above all, he was a man who was able to learn – and he did.

One of the most significant impacts on his behaviour was the outcome of three weeks we spent exploring the meaning and value of empathy. Some men had never heard the term and some said, once they understood what it meant, that they had never experienced it either by showing it or feeling that someone else had empathy for them. We would describe empathy as the ability to put oneself in someone else's shoes and thereby come to understand what they are feeling. Empathy is essential for a man who is abusing a family member. Salvatore's eventual grasp of empathy – which was a chal-lenge for many men over several weeks of work – meant that he became able to use that empathy in the group to the benefit of many men.

Showing empathy is critical, but allowing yourself to be vulnerable is also an essential part of the change process.

It was a major lesson for many men, and it had a great impact on their ability to understand how their family members may have been affected by their abuse. This understanding plays a critical role in motivating a man to cease his violent behaviour. It is also a tool to be used in communication, to show the person one is listening to that they have been heard and understood. I believe the development of empathy is another crucial step on the road to change.

The men's understanding of empathy was demonstrated in the group and Salvatore in particular was able to provide much comfort and positive reinforcement through his newfound capacity to empathise with others.

In the beginning, Salvatore's response to family members was reactive rather than a considered response designed to generate the best outcome. The reaction was frequently negative, and although he consciously changed it from being very loud to softer, it became just a different kind of aggression. Eventually, with the influence of concepts like empathy, Salvatore was able to consciously change his reactions to be well-considered responses. At first, responding takes more time, energy and thought than reaction, but the long-term benefits far outweigh the short-term consequences.

Salvatore found the distinction between empathy and sympathy particularly useful, explaining that he sees sympathy as taking a short time to express and empathy as an undertaking or commitment of time, be it short or extended, to another person. In other words, empathy is about giving the other person understanding and time. Without this, empathy would be of little value.

Clearly, it changed his way of communicating with his family members, who silently endorsed Salvatore's story despite a spelling mistake. What a change that must have been.

$$6$$

MATT

"Listen more before you go off your head, take note and relax." – Matt

When I arrived to interview Matt for this story, the first thing he did was to show me several pictures of his children. They were lovely photos and I was delighted to see them, and even more delighted to see the pride in Matt's face. I had seen him at his most miserable and it was great to see his joy.

He launched into answering my questions and telling his story without hesitation, and at no stage did I sense that he was holding back.

Matt had a great childhood. His mother worked hard to ensure he got everything he wanted, although he didn't appreciate that at the time. His happiest early memories are of riding his bike. Now, some forty years later, riding a bike of some kind is still one of his greatest pleasures. When he was a child he relished the sense of freedom riding gave him, as the concentration it took closed off his worries about other things. "There was no room for worries in my head when I was riding", he said.

His other worries as a child were the usual playmate issues

typical for his age and his concern for his mother, whom he watched for years as she was abused by his father. Matt felt impotent and unable to prevent the abuse taking place. His dad would come home drunk late at night, throw things at his mum and punch and hit her while using obscene language and putting her down.

Matt felt abused too by having to witness the violence towards his mother. His fear that she would be badly hurt resulted in him becoming something of a loner, refusing school camps and staying home to ensure his mum's safety. His whole life seemed to be overlaid by a cloud of fear and the need to protect her.

He knows she stayed in the relationship because she thought it was important for Matt and his siblings to have a father, but the time came when his father went too far and she left, taking the children with her. Matt's two older siblings left home and Matt, aged eleven, said he "felt an enormous sense of relief and freedom" creep up on him as he began to appreciate the fact that his Mum was now safe and he could relax and worry less about her.

It was later as a teenager when he was not achieving at school and constantly truanting that he started to treat his mother abusively. He left school in Year II with "a little bit of help from the school" and immediately started work as a labourer. He eventually secured a trade apprenticeship.

He continued to abuse his mother. He said, "I was angry with her for marrying Dad because that's why I turned out the way I did. It was her fault for marrying him". He would put her down using foul language, much as his father had done. In other words, he abused her severely on an emotional level without being physically violent.

Matt looks back on this now with great sorrow. I could see by the look on his face that he still feels shame for his treatment of his mum. He goes out of his way to ensure that his mum's current needs are met and has told his Mum how sorry he is many times. "I still find it hard to believe that I acted that way", he said. He has not seen his father for more than fifteen years, partially out of respect for his mother.

His mum had a happy childhood and was amazed that in both

her marriages she found herself abused physically and emotionally. It was only when Matt reached late teenage years that he recognised himself as like his dad and his anger grew.

Matt met his future wife at a nightclub. They both needed someone and "it just felt right to be together" he recalled. He loved her enthusiasm for getting ahead in life and her preparedness to work towards that end, as well as her moral values. She was also smart, he said, and although "she wouldn't win a beauty queen title it didn't matter because I was nothing much to look at myself" he added.

Matt said their life together was good in the years leading up to the birth of their first baby, an event which was celebrated with much joy by everyone. He helped a lot with their daughter and their marriage remained relatively stable until the birth of their second child. This was a traumatic birth in which the baby nearly died as the umbilical cord was round his neck and his wife nearly died from loss of blood.

"How did you react at this time" I asked him?

"Oh" he said airily, "I just took control as I usually do".

He ensured everyone's needs were met, talked with the doctors, calmed, soothed and organised whatever any family member needed. With his mother's help in caring for their daughter, the family survived the ordeal. But it was a dreadful experience for all involved and Matt's enormous fear about the potential deaths of his son or wife remained masked by his capacity to take control in a practical way.

It was after this that Matt started to feel something was slipping away from him. The two children required so much of his wife's attention. The baby had undefined problems and Matt's attempts to help were not appreciated, he thought. He felt useless and depressed. He started to become irritable and moody, taking offence easily and hitting back. He was starting to behave like his father had done, and recognising this made him even angrier.

He admits that he liked things being done his way. He describes himself as having tunnel vision and being unable to tolerate tasks being left incomplete or not done to his satisfaction. His behaviour was controlling. He used standover tactics to get his own way. When he didn't get what he wanted, he would storm out of the house. He now recognises how difficult he was to live with: demanding, demeaning and putting down his wife obscenely, losing his temper and yelling abuse at her and the children. He would also occasionally push his wife out of the way or throw something on the ground threateningly.

Losing his temper became an explosion that happened several times a day. Matt admits that he didn't always appreciate the impact it had on others until the next day. It happened at home but also on the road, at a restaurant and in other public places. He would loudly put down complete strangers, but be the first to protect an elderly or disabled person.

Matt was like this at work, but less so, which suggests he could control his outbursts. Nowadays he sometimes goes all day without losing it, and even though he believes he has reduced these outbursts by some fifty per cent, he still hasn't stopped. He can't explain why, but has sought counselling, which is in its early stages.

He says he doesn't like himself and can't remember ever doing so. He would like to find the nice Matt, the one of which he can be proud.

Matt described his wife and children's reaction. "They were terrified" he said. "They screwed up their faces and cringed in fear. They didn't go and hide because I saw the look on their faces and walked away thinking, 'I've got to get out of here. I'm scaring them. I'm a shit'".

He would behave this way over "stupid little things". Matt describes it as a toxic relationship. Finally, he threw his wife out of the house following an altercation, gave her the car keys and locked the door on her. She returned later with family members to get the children and took out an intervention order against Matt a few weeks later. This prevented contact with her or the children until the court hearing some eight months later.

Matt apologised to his wife for his behaviour soon after the breakup. Together they explained to the children that Mummy and Daddy couldn't live together anymore because Daddy would get angry with Mummy and that was not nice for Mummy or the children. His relationship with her now is less combative, but limited. Matt thinks she's unsure whether she can really trust him yet. This he understands.

Matt was devastated, not only at losing contact with his children, but also because it was the result of his own actions which he knew were wrong, although at that stage he did not understand the full impact of his behaviour or how to stop it. A friend who had attended the Men's Behaviour Change Program recommended it to Matt, who went to a doctor and then straight to the program, where he was interviewed for his suitability to join and was accepted.

He attended the twenty-week program and then, at the suggestion of his facilitator, he joined the group that followed it, which worked with men to sustain change and continue growth.

Matt found it difficult to attend regularly or with great motivation as he found it exhausting after a day's work that usually finished late. He didn't always feel like coming, particularly if his behaviour had recently been controlling and abusive. If a man behaved abusively at home he sometimes felt too embarrassed to admit it in group and so avoidance became the preferred option. However, with some encouragement Matt stayed and found that his learning increased.

The very first thing that Matt said helped him change was "thought stopping" and the "5 x 5" rule. In brief, this involves asking yourself whether this will matter in five minutes, five hours, five days, five weeks, five months or five years. The hardest part of this strategy is the ability to stop the negative thinking that is accumulating, but thought stopping and asking oneself these questions often highlights that the trigger that could lead to violence or abuse was in fact a petty matter.

Matt also said that learning the vocabulary and terminology that was used in discussions about family violence was of great value as it opened his eyes and increased his understanding of what constituted violence and how it could be controlled. It helped him identify harmful things he was doing and which he had previously failed to recognise. I felt for him as I understood that not knowing what it is that you don't know is a very difficult place to learn from. Discovering that you have been doing something that brought on a sense of shame was a confronting lesson. I admired him for sticking with it.

He also said, "Hearing other men speak about their abuse and violence made me feel less alone". He eventually valued the comradeship of the other men and the support he received from them and gradually he was able to make small changes in his behaviour.

When looking back over his treatment of his family members his view of himself "disgusted" him and he practised other ways of behaving.

He started noticing situations in which he would once have reacted violently, and was considering different ways of responding. "Sometimes my brain would go numb and I would snap and the old Matt would appear", he said. He gradually trained himself to contain his anger a little more and respond in considered and non-threatening, rather than reactionary, way. He was able to do this successfully, but not all the time, so while improvement was noted, Matt still had a way to go.

An example of change he gave was a recent incident in which his young son spoke rudely and abusively to him. Matt would once have hurled foul abuse back at the boy, but this time he crouched down to his son's level, gently held him in his arms and, looking him in the eye, said quietly, "Daddy feels really sad when you say that because it isn't true". His son responded with "Okay Dad" and the episode was over. Matt's mother commented on how differently he handled his son compared with the past and Matt was pleased.

Matt feels most worried that he may react badly these days when he is very tired. Fortunately his self-awareness has grown significantly and he can recognise these vulnerable times and take a nap or do something that relaxes him, such as go for a ride or tinker with the car he is painstakingly restoring. This is helping, but he is not yet able to fully control all his behaviour no matter how unjustified he recognises it to be.

Matt said he has even got the message that the dog does not like being shouted at, so his sound level has greatly reduced and his out-of-control reactions have decreased somewhat.

He introduced his dog, Jacky, to me and she pranced excitedly around us with her tail wagging at a great rate and I'm sure it was a smile on her face. This was mirrored by Matt, who was talking animatedly with a smile on his face to the dog he obviously loved. It was a pleasure to watch.

"At times I still blurt out what I think", Matt said. His friend suggested recently that maybe Matt's son's autism had come from Matt, and that perhaps he should by tested by a specialised psychologist. Matt now has an appointment to check that out. I asked him how he would feel if he was found to be on the spectrum and he responded, "I would be relieved because we would know what the problem is instead of just guessing. I think it would clarify things for us. I know it could be that my son inherited it from me, because I was a pretty crummy student".

Matt was finally allowed access to the children at the court case which dealt with the intervention order. This made him very happy. But some time later an incident which he claims was accidental appeared violent and frightening to the children, so he was denied access again.

Matt was quite depressed and unable to do anything about it. He gave up, at least temporarily, too scared to hope any more for fear it would be in vain. "Coming to group was hard", he said. He felt shame for his actions that, although unintentional, had caused this break from his parenting role. It was some months before he was allowed to see his children again. The reunion with his son was great and the relationship flourishes, but his daughter does not want to see him yet and neither child wants to come to the house which holds such unpleasant memories for them. Matt understands this and although it makes him sad that his daughter doesn't want to see him, he understands why. "I know where she's coming from", he said, "because that's how I felt with my dad".

Recently both his mother and a long-term mate complimented him on his changed behaviour. I asked if they would consider writing a paragraph to that effect. Matt gave me their phone numbers with their okay. I asked his permission to ask certain questions of them and Matt's response was, "Yes I'm an open book, anything that helps the future of men being kind to women instead of abusive is okay by me."

Both Matt and an ex-girlfriend with whom I spoke agree that there is more work to be done. Matt has significantly reduced his out-of-control, abusive behaviour, but he still chooses to behave that way at times and girlfriends/partners are generally the most likely to be exposed to it. He is still horrified at his previous behaviour and, as with all tasks of any size, Matt is determined to finish the job he has started, of changing from a man with toxic behaviour to a man who hurts no one, a man of whom he can be proud.

Susan, Matt's mother

After my time with Matt I called Matt's mum, who was quite prepared to speak unreservedly with me, which I greatly appreciated. Yes, she had noticed a big difference in Matt. He used to have such a temper, but now he controls it a lot more. She recalled her happy childhood and the marriages that had such a negative impact on her children. She told me of her pride in Matt's behaviour with his son and commented that she was very impressed that when he last picked up his son for access, Matt complemented his ex-wife on the way she was raising the children. Susan was a proud mum and she said happily, "Matt gives terrific hugs".

Ben, Matt's mate

I also called Matt's mate who had recently praised Matt for "keeping his cool" instead of "losing it". He said enthusiastically that the change in his very old friend Matt had been terrific. He said the change was from "dramatic and foul-mouthed yelling, abusing and generally going off his head" to "mellow, chilled-out and altogether a different person who didn't lose his cool so much anymore". He said that he thought the group Matt attended had helped a lot and that Matt was a different man. He had changed and was easier to be around. When I asked for an example, Ben told me that he and Matt recently bought a coffee and Matt's coffee was not what he had ordered. Once upon a time he would have sworn loudly, strode into the shop noisily and embarrassingly demanded a replacement coffee. This time he just said "whatever" and drank it. Ben was impressed.

I thanked Ben. After we had hung up he sent me the following message.

"Hi. I just thought that Matt's a lot more open now about his feelings and he doesn't mind bringing things up to get them off his chest. This had been good for me as well.

Thanks, Ben"

Steve, work colleague

I have worked with Matt for nearly six years and I have seen great changes. He used to lose his temper so badly he would throw a ladder and would always bite back if in any way provoked. Now he ignores the things that used to trigger him and sometimes just walks away for a few minutes before returning to talk.

His biggest downfall nowadays is being brutally honest, telling people what they don't want to hear. He has a heart of gold and is very generous but his honesty is abusive at times. I have felt belittled by it. Choosing better words to communicate with is what he needs to work on now.

Matt hides his feelings a lot and I think he needs to talk about them more.

Margaret says ...

Matt's story about how far he has come is a wonderful source of inspiration for further change. Seeking his recent ex-girlfriend's opinion and agreeing with it stands him in good stead for finishing the change he has started. He is rightly proud of what he has achieved so far and is painfully honest about what still needs to be done.

Matt's reluctance to attend group after he had behaved abusively is shared by many men. The very time that they need the group most is the hardest time to attend. Once again, shame gets in the way. Matt seemed to take a while to trust the group and his participation varied according to his levels of tiredness and motivation. He nearly pulled out on one or two occasions, but with a little gentle nudging he returned. As he said, he doesn't like to leave a job unfinished. However, there came a point when he seemed to visibly relax and talk openly, as if he had decided that he had to make the most of this opportunity. And he did.

Relapse is common in any attempt at changing old habits and behaviour, be they smoking, eating chocolate or walking with your hands in your pockets. In Matt's case, there is little distinction between describing his behaviour as relapsing or regarding it as unfinished change. Either way, the group spends time exploring relapse prevention in order to protect anyone who may be vulnerable at this point. Strategies suggested differ from one man to another as there is no magic wand to be waved to protect women and children. The men know what works best for them.

One aspect of this work that inspired me to continue working with the men was the stories some would tell of their attempts to influence other men. This was one of the goals of the group, and something Matt was really good at. He would regale us with tales of how he told a mate who was going through a hard time that he couldn't treat his wife like that, it was just not okay. He would worry about their behaviour and seek support in working out how best to handle them. He had no trouble speaking his mind to other men who he thought were harming their partners, but was never inappropriately blunt or rude in the group. Men helping other men is a great outcome of the program. Its effectiveness increases as the men demonstrate the changes they have made.

I asked Matt if he remembered any of the quotes we had discussed in the group, or if he had a favourite. He replied that he had forgotten them but I could include, "Listen more before you go off your head, take note and relax". So a new relevant and pithy quote from Matt heads his story.

MARK

"Vulnerability is not weakness. It is our most important measure of courage."

– Brené Brown

I have never worked with Mark. I had seen him around, particularly in his capacity as a volunteer with young people, and I knew he had completed the first Men's Behaviour Change Program the agency had conducted, around twenty-five years ago. I was surprised at the alacrity with which he agreed to have his story written, given that he barely knew me.

I was also grateful that he trusted me with his personal story. My curiosity was aroused when he started by saying how loved and adored by his parents he was and what good parents they were. This was a little different from most of the other stories I had heard or read.

~

MARK WAS BORN IN MELBOURNE, the youngest of six children to "older Dutch Catholic" parents. They adored Mark. He could do no wrong, and if he did, it became the source of amusement rather than discipline or punishment. He was confident at home and felt well-loved and even idolised. He received a lot of praise. He became his dad's shadow, following him around, enjoying his company and helping him with various tasks.

His sister did not fare so well. She had quite a temper and was often hit by their dad in his effort to control her behaviour. Mark assumed this was totally his sister's fault and that she was the cause of his father's outbursts. She was clearly the problem; his father was not.

At the age of nine, Mark became an uncle and the family grew and grew. He continued to feel loved within his large family unit.

He learned to speak both English and Dutch which was the predominant language used at home, but his English vocabulary was sparse and his communication skills problematic as he didn't always express himself clearly or to his advantage in English.

He also developed a fear of being picked on because of his Dutch surname, which he went to some lengths to avoid mentioning whenever possible. Although his fear was never realised, it remained with him for a long time.

School, however, was a different matter. Although he was a bright boy, his poor communication disadvantaged him and his first two days at school earned him the strap on both days. The first day it was for laughing when the nun's robe became caught in a desk, and the second when he refused to go into the convent next door to retrieve the hat that he had thrown over the fence while being bullied.

School did not improve and by Grade 1 he started wagging. He, and at times two of his older sisters, would hide under the pine trees in fine weather and in the hayshed on cold, wet days. This plan was going quite smoothly until the local shopkeeper, whom they had visited during school hours, told their older brother about these visits. The wagging ended there.

Frequent changes of school due to his father's ill health meant that school was never a comfortable or safe place for Mark, although he finished with good results at the end of Year 11.

Mark became an apprentice. His school life had left Mark low in confidence and anxious about his ability to fit in. He recalls being so nervous that he spent much time at work praying that he would not make a mistake. He won awards and was awarded his apprenticeship in three years instead of four, but he spent the entire three years feeling anxious about his performance, despite the high standard he achieved.

Around this time, Mark started to assert his independence by going out a lot more, refusing to speak Dutch at home and rejecting anything to do with his Dutch heritage.

Once qualified he obtained a job in Queensland which, Mark said, broke his parents' hearts, although they believed he would not be gone for long. The job worked out well, and Mark kept it for six years.

He had no life skills apart from cleaning, which he had done at home. He learned to cook. He started drinking and, to fit in and become accepted, became something of a show-off. Mark commented that in Queensland, as in all other jobs he had had, he was fortunate to have good employers. He also had a good work ethic and produced high-quality outcomes.

One day, one of his work colleagues visited and brought his sister with him. She needed somewhere to live, so she rented a room from Mark until she went away with her boyfriend. That relationship ended and she returned to Mark's house, ill and alone. Mark felt sorry for her, and over time, they built a relationship and became a couple. During the next year or two they got to know each other's strengths and foibles, along with some of their childhood history.

Pam was suffering from post-traumatic stress disorder, PTSD, due to severe abuse as a child and was low in trust and confidence. Mark, on the other hand, was initially confident but describes himself as "emotionally immature and hence detached" and on reflection greatly regrets his inability to empathise with Pam or give her the care she needed.

Mark had been a people-pleaser all his life. He was discovering for the first time that this approach was not working with Pam. He tried harder and harder and still it was not working. His anger grew until he was holding it tightly inside.

"We did have a lot of fun", he said, "and I always had faith that it would work out. But I couldn't handle it if she wouldn't talk to me or if she went away for a few days after disagreements. Over time, the length of silence became longer for what seemed to be trivial matters. As a result, I started to feel like a victim. I also couldn't cope with criticism, especially if it was in front of others. I would withdraw, become very quiet and just bottle my feelings up. In retrospect, I can see that I was brought up with few boundaries and no criticism, so I had no idea how to handle it. My thinking mirrored that of my view of my sister. She was the problem, not me."

While the marriage was deteriorating, Mark's father died. Mark could have visited him shortly before his death, but under the impression that his dad's health having improved, Mark kept working. He was later devastated to realise that he had once again put work before family, a choice he regrets making many times over in that period of his life.

Mark said his sadness was "enormous" and he couldn't stop crying and also couldn't express his grief in words. Slowly that grief turned to anger, which he buried inside him along with the other buried feelings and "gradually life began to unravel", he said.

"I was in the throes of starting up my own business", said Mark. "I was needed at home to care for my daughter while Pam had postnatal depression. I was feeling very stressed."

Mark and Pam moved back to Melbourne and the friction between them escalated. Mark started to abuse Pam by yelling, sulking and physically pushing her.

Pam became pregnant and Mark was unable to see that she was terrified. She didn't want a girl, but she gave birth to a daughter and suffered postnatal depression for some time afterwards. This depression included some serious, life-threatening behaviour which led to hospitalisation and enormous stress for both Pam and Mark.

Back home again, the relationship did not improve. Mark continued pushing Pam, shouting abuse. In the last incident, in front of his daughter then aged about six, Mark smashed his dinner plate on the kitchen floor then walked into the living room where he threw Pam's food over her with significant force and yelled at her abusively. He said, "I lost complete control". His daughter cried uncontrollably and ran next door in fear. Pam decided to leave the marriage.

"I did not want this to happen and although Pam and my daughter left, I sought marriage counselling and we both attended. My plan was to gather strategies to put in place to save the marriage. I still had no idea how much I contributed to its demise."

Although they separated, the marriage became more conflicted. Both Mark and Pam were angry at the way life had turned out and each was unclear how it happened or how it could be repaired.

Mark sought help through the Men's Behaviour Change Program, where his goal was to fully justify that he was not the problem in his marriage.

As is the agency's policy, wives and partners were contacted during this time to check on their wellbeing. In one such conversation, Pam told the caller that she did not believe that Mark could ever change. The twenty-week program finished with Mark still believing Pam was at fault, that she was the problem. At no time did Mark take responsibility for his contribution to the marriage breakdown.

Pam told Mark that he was "like Martin Bryant", perpetrator of the infamous Port Arthur massacre. Mark agrees that he recalls an incident shortly afterwards when he was full of silent rage. "I was ready to do major damage", he said.

I asked Mark what stopped him from doing so and he said simply, "It wasn't the man that I wanted to be, and I didn't want to let down the people who were supporting me at the agency where I completed the program. They believed in me".

Mark started volunteer work with young people, and the relationships he built there showed him the importance of respect, trust and taking responsibility for one's own behaviour, regardless of provocation. He got to the stage where he could take responsibility for his behaviour, but not yet publicly.

He also connected with one of the facilitators outside the agency and a friendship developed. It was a tremendous help in moving Mark further towards owning his behaviour. Mark and the facilitator shared many discussions, including examining Mark's shadow or his "dark side". Mark describes this as the side of a person that lies unacknowledged, hidden behind shame or denial. This was a great help to him and increased his capacity to recognise, at least silently, what his contribution to the marriage had been and how damaging his behaviour had been.

The facilitator also taught Mark how to listen, even when he didn't want to hear what was being said, but because it was important for the other person to verbalise it. This listening was referred to by another staff member as "sitting in a prickly pair of pants". It is uncomfortable for the listener, but is done out of empathy for the person needing to speak.

He joined the follow-up group, which contributed to his growing emotional maturity over the four years he attended, and he joined another men's group which provided him with further opportunities to talk. In both groups, he learned from facilitators and other men who were further down the track than he was.

Mark looks back with deep regret at his total lack of awareness as a young man, his need to invest so much time and energy into creating a mask which would ensure he was accepted in society and satisfy his ego, and his failure to be able to adequately express his needs in a way that meant others could understand him.

He remains appalled at the damage he has done to his ex-wife and his daughter. He has apologised and done all he can to create a healthy relationship with them both.

Mark says that on reflection, his anger dissipated in the early stages of his change process, but being able to state what his worst behaviour had been like and own it did not come for many years. When it did, forgiving his ex-wife and himself came easily, and his anger was replaced with compassion for Pam and his daughter.

Although she was in another state, he made attempts to support Pam, but they were not successful. His contact with his daughter, also living in another state, was spasmodic. When it did happen, they were able to talk about the past without rancour and it felt healthy to Mark. He thought she felt the same, but there are long periods where he has response from her at all.

Mark was in another relationship for many years. Despite tensions, he never resorted to abusive behaviour of any kind.

While he deeply regrets his behaviour and the damage he caused over eight years of abusive behaviour towards Pam, Mark now recognises that the work he has done since then has made him a different person, a man that he now likes and can see becoming an even better man as he continues to work on himself.

Without the work he has done he would not have grown as he has. He would not have the level of self-awareness he now appreciates. He would not be able to communicate as well as he can now. He would not have gained insight into his "dark side" and learned to manage it successfully. Above all, he would not have the excellent friends and relationships he now enjoys.

Every birthday he celebrates alone, finding a special place in the bush to sit and reflect on the past year. After this annual self-inspection, he selects those aspects that he would like to improve on in the year to come.

Acknowledging his greatest weaknesses freed Mark to examine his life regularly, with honesty and determination to continue seeking his best self.

Margaret says ...

Mark's is a sad story within the setting of strong and perpetually supportive and loving parents and family life. The truth of the quote at the start of his story is evident throughout his journey. Only after Mark fully recognised and publicly acknowledged his "weakness" could real change occur.

Lack of self-awareness and naivety play such a significant role in lives that can be transformed with the determination and the opportunity to grow in emotional intelligence. Mark's journey has been long, and continues, as I believe the journey of every person who has the courage to examine their life does.

Changing behaviour that is the result of deep-rooted repressed emotions is not a task that can be completed in six or twenty weeks, or even six or twenty months. Change is incremental, and the same experience examined at different stages of one's life can reveal new insights, so that in old age our view of a specific experience may have changed dramatically.

Mark's changes seem to have been brought about in four different settings. Behind him was a backdrop of much love from his parents, who continued to love him throughout their lives.

Mark's friendship with a facilitator and their shared, intimate one-on-one conversations played a significant role in his change. Here was someone with whom Mark could be authentic, someone he trusted to see the dark side of him, someone he could empty those repressed feelings onto, and someone who would challenge him. What a treasure.

Mark then found that group work was also useful, because the learning was shared. Other men who had also been violent or abusive had stories and insights that Mark could learn from, and he could contribute some of his learnings to them. The group gave him a sense of belonging, a place of safety, somewhere he could be the real Mark.

Mark worked for years with youths who had their own anger challenges. In this environment, he earned the trust of the youth as well as his colleagues, and he was able to use some of his learnings in his work with the boys, a perfectly reciprocal arrangement.

8

———

JORDON

"It is what it is – or is it?" – Jordon

Whho en I met Jordon to hear his story, I was delighted by how much he had to say. Clearly, he had been listening in the group and developing a higher level of emotional intelligence than I was aware of. I was impressed by his learning.

JORDON HAD a happy childhood surrounded by a close-knit group of family and friends. Both his parents and his grandparents were always present. Although not financially well off, they were comfortable. Only now, while reflecting on his past, is he thinking about what he would like to do differently as a parent and how his upbringing affected the man he became. Jordon also wonders what influence, if any, his Chilean heritage may have had on him. His grandparents were "hot-headed", he said.

Jordon is not blaming in any way. He is simply examining his life and learning from his experiences.

I don't hold anything against anyone, but now I'm more balanced in my thinking, and I realise that punishment without any explanation of what has been done wrong or why it is wrong is less than useful. I would get belted for something, often without any understanding of what I had done wrong, and I learned that life was that way and I accepted it, at least superficially.

My sister developed better ways to manage stress than I did. I always thought that you simply fought fire with another fire. I wish I had been educated emotionally. I wish I had been taught how to be a man instead of just being told that men don't cry. Although I had a sister and cousins, there was no one my age to compare with and so I accepted life as it was. "It is what it is" was my way of thinking.

I now understand that the first child is like a trial run, when as a parent you do a lot of learning. The second child has more freedom, I think. Anyway, my sister grew up with a closer relationship with my parents. It was more trusting and therefore more intimate. But I still love my parents too.

I finished Year 12 in trade school and became a carpenter, which I am happy doing most of the time. Occasionally I feel like going back and training for something else and I wouldn't mind teaching carpentry. At times I feel like I have some knowledge to share and at other times I don't. But I do think I have developed some wisdom over the years, which was helped by the group work during which I have become more emotionally mature.

As a kid I got angry easily. I was a sore loser. At sixteen, I would smash the remote when playing video games if they weren't working out as I wanted.

I met my first girlfriend, Wendy, in Year 7. When we were eighteen and twenty, she became pregnant. We decided to go ahead and have the baby. That is when my personal issues came to the surface. We were staying in a bungalow at Mum and Dad's house. We would argue constantly about money. I had just started my apprenticeship. We also spent much time at her parents' home. Altogether there was a lot of fighting, and I became disrespectful towards people.

After the birth of our daughter we enjoyed a brief honeymoon period, but I got fed up with the screaming baby and I hit my girlfriend across the body. She said she couldn't breastfeed our baby after that.

It scared me and I felt like a monster. After that our relationship was off and on. When it was back on, we never dealt with the issues that had led to us separating, so the cycle continued. Things got worse. I couldn't deal with any kind of criticism. I would react with verbal abuse and later physical abuse, that included pushing, grabbing, punching and biting.

I would know I was getting uptight when my jaw clenched, my fists clenched and my whole body tightened, but I didn't know then what my body was telling me or what to do about it. I didn't like myself and I knew this couldn't continue, so I told Wendy to leave and she and my daughter moved to a country town.

I saw them most weekends. During that time, we both developed drug habits. I went right out of control. We continued our on-again-off again relationship until she eventually moved back to her mum's house and I to my mum's. I lied about my drug use, I lied about my intentions with Wendy, I barely talked to my family, and I smashed up my room and other parts of the house on a regular basis. I also met my current partner, Kim, during that time and she became pregnant.

Meanwhile, my family had had enough of my out-of-control behaviour and the police arrested me on three occasions. Subsequently I had two intervention orders taken out against me to prevent me from going near my parents.

The third incident started with me having a car accident when visiting my then ex-partner, Wendy, and a drug-fuelled fight ensued. Despite the current intervention order, I went home to my parents' house following the fight with the best of intentions not to cause problems. However, I ended up wrestling with my dad and breaking my sister's tooth.

The police were called. I was taken not to the local lock-up but to remand. I was allowed one call, so I called my grandparents. Grandma cried. I felt terrible, and went back to my cell and cried too. I was lucky. Another inmate saw my distress and became a very caring friend to me during my time there. There were some good men in remand, believe it or not. It took a few days to get over the shock of being in there. I was back in court ten days later. I was optimistic because I knew I was an okay guy underneath and I just needed to learn how to handle myself better.

My father, grandfather and my sister were in court, but I just couldn't look at them. My shame was enormous. I just wanted to hide. I was not released. I was sent back to remand. At that announcement my world sort of ended. Remand is not fun, but it is a good way to stop you in your tracks. You have a lot of time to think. It was here that I finally came to the conclusion that I was an idiot.

It was another week before going to court again. I went to church within the prison, and I did lots of thinking. I knew I was an idiot, but I didn't know how to fix me. The court took care of that. I got a corrections order which included eight weeks of drug counselling, and then attendance at the Men's Behaviour Change Program. I was open to learning how to break the cycle. I like this quote, although I don't know its source, but it does sum up my cycle: "The definition of madness is doing the same thing over and over and expecting a different outcome."

The same people were at court the second time, my father, sister and grandfather. My partner, Kim, who had given birth to our son, was also present. After court I lived with my grandparents for a few months before they threw me out for using drugs again. I went to live with Kim. We are still together. I stopped using drugs. I stopped losing my temper. I rarely drink. I still have times when I feel a surge of energy that needs releasing and I do so in ways that harm no one, like throwing a soccer ball against the wall or giving my punch bag a hard time. I never get physical with anyone and am never deliberately verbally abusive. I do need to work on the language I use. My choice of words can be offensive. I am still a bit rough around the edges, but I used to be a ball of destructive anger.

I have decided to go to a psychologist to get help to release that energy in a positive way and I attend the group that follows the Men's Behaviour Change Program.

All the programs I have been involved in have helped me change. Early in the first one I sat and thought to myself, "You know what? This makes a lot of sense".

I learned that I've got to learn to take it, whatever "it" is. I am learning that it's okay to agree to disagree and I don't need to take the attitude that it's my way or else.

I like the 5 x 5 rule, which requires me to stop and ask myself if this will matter in five minutes, five hours, five days and so on, but I've got to learn to put the brakes on first. If you don't take that moment to stop and think, you've lost it.

I've learned that I need to look after myself, get enough sleep, eat properly, avoid things or people that are not good for me, and take notice of symptoms that may tell me that tension is building.

I think empathy is important. I know how I like to feel understood, and I can now use it to communicate better with others.

And finally, it is reassuring to know that a certain group of men that I trust is there for me to reach out to as often as I need.

My parents and other family members are very relieved. They were frightened and very worried that I was on the wrong road for good. It was hard for them, because I was their son and they struggled to avoid me even when it was in their best interests to do so.

I don't see my ex-partner Wendy nowadays, but I think I will write her a letter apologising for my past behaviour. She was certainly hurt by me and at times scared of me.

My current partner, Melanie, has been a bit frightened and at times hurt and offended by what I have said. She knows what I was like. I wonder if she has an image of me as a monster still lurking in the background? That is an awful thought to me.

I have three children. Two are mine and one is a stepson. I love them all. My daughter lives with my parents and I see her a lot. She is the most affected by my past behaviour. She sees or senses my tension and worries that I might lose it. I carefully spell out to her that it is okay to feel angry and to give an opinion, but it is not okay to lose it.

I have put a lot of people though immense stress. I take responsibility for that. They are happy about where I have got to. I am happy to be where I am today. I intend to keep growing and getting rid of any doubts anyone has about my future behaviour.

Margaret says …

Jordon was one of the youngest and quietest in the group. so it was difficult to know how much progress he was making. His story has taken care of that, and both the reader and I can see how much he has grown emotionally.

Jordon mentioned that he might write a letter of apology to his ex-partner Wendy. The group worked on this subject, exploring together what makes an apology authentic and ensuring that it is being written for the right reasons. It was agreed that an apology should expect no reply and should state clearly and specifically just what behaviour is being referred to with no "buts", no minimisation and no excuses. It should also acknowledge the hurt and fear experienced by the person receiving the apology, and include a promise not to behave that way again. This promise needs to be backed up by a plan that removes or reduces the risk of future violent and abusive behaviour.

Some men have written such a letter, sometimes checked by the group before it is sent to ensure it meets the criteria discussed. Some men have received responses, both positive and negative, and some have received no response at all. The men are faced with the reality that it may take a long time for trust or forgiveness to occur, or it may never occur. That is, of course, the other person's prerogative.

After group work, one-on-one therapy or both, it may be that the man and his wife or partner grow closer, as happened in some cases, or move further apart as their personal growth and life experiences take them in a similar direction at a different rate or in completely different directions. Some men share the learning with their partners, and in some cases the partners do not want to know what the men are learning about.

9

KEVIN

"No buts." – Kevin

Kevin wrote his story soon after the idea of doing so was shared with the group members. The book's title, *No Buts*, was borrowed from Kevin's story with his permission. It is intrinsic to the change process. If buts are allowed, no change is possible.

AT FIRST GLANCE, I seem a very laid-back, relaxed, gentle, almost mild guy. I went along with that illusion, even though I knew my childhood had left me with a few emotional scars and triggers that I thought would disappear in time if I hid them. Anger with my mother, her coldness and religious strictness for instance, the narrow, male-dominated education system I grew up in, my insecurity with women, for example. I thought all that would fade away in time. I grew up in England in the 1960s at a time when we believed anything was possible.

So through my teenage years I seemed to cope okay. I was popular with girls, good at school, good at sport, and particularly musical. It was only when I got married much later that I knew there were some insecurities, some mysteries, some discrepancies in my story which hadn't been admitted. Perhaps they would disappear.

Years later, after coming to Australia, I thought marriage to a kind and beautiful girl would finally solve everything and keep all those doubts about what and who I was safely locked inside of me. Two lovely daughters and a home in the hills above Melbourne came along.

But of course, a few years later, with two kids, a single income as a schoolteacher, and with life's road becoming a little bumpier, I finally resorted to the angry, resentful, self-pitying child that was the other side of my double-sided coin. Money matters, my old insecurity, mistrust and resentments started to reappear. My father, who in later life became a real friend, passed away suddenly and at about that time I started to get depressed and anxious. And of course I began to take out the insecurity and injustice I felt on my wife.

So what did I do? I blew up at her on the streets of a foreign city because I thought she had paid too much for ice creams for the children, who cowered behind her. I threw a mug against the wall when she suggested we move house. I shouted at my daughter when she wouldn't drink a glass of orange juice. I shouted at my wife as she lay in the bathtub, trying to get away from me. And every time my outburst would be followed by days of seething anger, sadness and confusion. It took me a long time to admit it was self-pity.

My temper, tantrums and angry outbursts were justified, weren't they? An attempt at marriage counselling just gave me more scope to vent my anger. I was mystified that the counsellor didn't take my side. When she addressed my behaviour I just began my defence with "but...".

My wife later asked me to leave the family home, so bad was my behaviour. "But ... I'm a good man ..." I replied, outraged again at the unfairness of it all.

My wife had not completely rejected me, though I moved out. Thanks to a friend, I found a place to stay not far away. Hurt though I was, it was impossible not to admit that something was wrong. So I began my first men's behaviour change group as part of a bargain to try and save the marriage. Little did I know how it would change me, turning me inside out, forcing me to see my other side which I had tried so hard to deny and conceal.

Of course this didn't happen straightaway. My first meeting, as well as the weeks before it, were filled with fear and trepidation. A fear of what I didn't know, but that's what fear is. Somehow I knew there might be pain or shame, but maybe, just maybe, there was something in me that might just get fixed if I had the courage to share with other men.

Other men? At first it seemed a bit daunting, opening yourself up to a dozen or so sitting in a circle. Soon after I discovered how well other men could help. You see, I'd tried counsellors and therapists for years, but when a man in the group looked across at me and told me the things I needed to hear about myself, exactly when I needed to hear them, in words so direct I couldn't argue with them, and an honesty that couldn't be denied, that was when the men's group started to work.

The next step was hearing about the "victim hole", which was exactly where I was sitting at the time and then the "cycle of violence." This cycle resonated with me as it described the stages many men go through as their anger escalates and they become abusive or violent before feeling remorse and trying to make up for the behaviour, after which the cycle starts again. A veil was lifted and revealed what my tangled emotions of resentment and self-pity were all about. "Family of origin" came next and more exploration into emotions, thoughts and attitudes that had been locked away for years.

It was as if I was finally forced to drop the false image so carefully constructed over a lifetime and come down to earth and join the other men on the course. They could see who I was and I learned to trust them. They turned out to be the best friends a man could ever have.

"So I turned myself to face me" is a David Bowie lyric, and that is exactly what I was forced to do for the first time in my life. And strangely enough, things started to work out better. My wife could see I was making an effort, but there was more to it than that. I discovered what it was like to come out from behind my wall of defence, to tear down the image I had tried so vainly to keep up, to admit my failings and, with the help of the honest and perceptive men in the groups I attended, I became more receptive, more forgiving of myself and others. I became more human. I slowly accepted both sides of myself. No more "buts".

It didn't come easy, maybe ten years of listening, learning, rejecting old patterns of thought, expectations and habits. But thanks to the men who walked that road with me, I came out as a whole human being. No more hiding or denying my faults. I listened when they pointed out things I said or did which I was trying to whitewash. No more "buts".

A few years ago I heard a talk on the radio on Indigenous languages. There is no Aboriginal word for "but". Things are either there or they're not. It took the Men's Program for me to admit I was wrong, flawed, angry and destructive of those around me. That was the first step in putting things right. I'm still working on it, but at least I'm moving forward. No more "buts".

Margaret says …

Kevin's description of himself is a great reflection on his time in the group and highlights his wise and insightful understanding of his journey.

There is a story about a man who goes for the same walk each day and falls in the same hole each time. He awkwardly clambers out with great effort and resumes his walk, only to repeat the same thing the next day. He frequently complains about this hole and feels sorry for himself for having to endure constant falls. He becomes angry that no one takes responsibility for filling the hole in, and somehow it keeps getting deeper. Eventually, after many falls and overcoming many challenges to climb out of the hole, the man sidesteps the hole on his walks. In time he takes to walking on different streets where there are no holes to fall into.

This story reflects Kevin's journey. When he left the group due to a move far away, he was missed because he went to great lengths to gain the maximum learning from the group and had become an integral part of it over some eighteen months. He brought stories of the victim holes he fell into to the group, and we groaned with him. He brought stories of holes avoided, and we celebrated with him. He told his story openly and honestly to men who he rightly thought may benefit from hearing it. He fell into the holes less and less often, until he came to group with much less to say about his journey and more to offer others. This is the road many men travel in the change process. It is this mixture of experience and learning that ensures the group remains vibrant and full of learning opportunities of all kinds.

"Victim hole" is a term used to describe a time or place in which a person feels and acts like a victim, blaming others for his behaviour and taking no responsibility for it at all. It is a way of avoiding shame. Many men start the Men's Behaviour Change Program feeling this way, as well as angry that they should be expected to shoulder responsibility for behaviour that was "not their fault". Some of these men bring remnants of victim thinking to the second group where all group members can help them to climb out of that hole. And help they do.

Kevin learned about "no buts" the hard way, having had to dismantle a wall in order to get to his real feelings and thoughts. We all have walls. Some are necessary, some are temporary, and many are built by men who have been taught that real men neither show nor discuss their feelings. Where else to put them but behind a wall where they could be hidden from others and so often from themselves also?

"Buts" is an apt term for excuses, or what we often refer to as smokescreens. They are statements and thoughts that take responsibility for the abusive action away from the perpetrator and deflect it elsewhere. This helps the perpetrator avoid doing anything to remedy the situation or prevent it from happening again. Sometimes it can be difficult for either the perpetrator or the victim to see what is really happening and who is really responsible. The group can, and does, pick up when the word "but" is used to avoid responsibility.

10

PETE

"I'm a Pom with a calm and gentle nature and incredible strength of mind and determination.

I emigrated to Australia in 2010 after growing up in a small village in West Sussex, England. It was a very quiet and peaceful start, during a very much more relaxed time compared to now. This village was beautiful, picturesque. Everybody knew each other not just by sight but by name.

My household consisted of my mother and stepfather, three siblings and me. The extended family – grandparents, aunts, uncles, cousins, nieces and nephews – lived within walking distance. My family was incredibly co-dependent. We seemed to survive on inter-family discourse, and we always had very firm views on how others should lead their lives, in hindsight with very little self-awareness.

It was a long distance from a family with very strong morals, values and views. It was predominantly matriarchal with a weak patriarchal input. The men in the family were generally people pleasers and would do anything for a quiet life. I too adopted this way of being. During the last few years, through deep inner work and growing self-awareness, I have reflected on my upbringing and how it influenced and shaped the choices I made in my life, the interpersonal relationships I formed and the way I chose to behave.

Growing up I had few adult males as good general role models, except for my stepdad, who had a very strong work ethic. He had a full-time job, but also worked many hours in the evenings and weekends as a gardener.

My high school years were mainly a continuation of the early years, but due to increased academic work and a few dominant male friends from whom I received some emotional bullying, I started to play truant by deliberately missing the school bus about a mile from my home.

I will never forget the last time that I walked back into the family home and, seeing my mother in the kitchen, I said very sheepishly, "I missed the bus". In exasperation, my mother proceeded to throw the kitchen furniture at me. In between dodging crockery and stools coming at me, I ultimately realised I was on my own with my bullying problem, just as I was alone with feeling overwhelmed by the amount of work that was coming my way. That meant only I could deal with it.

I had to get back to school and I did, though I was behind in my learning. I was head down and bum up for the last years of my high school and I successfully passed all my exams. In hindsight, this is where my work ethic originated. I was very proud of what I had succeeded in doing.

I started my work career on the day of my fourteenth birthday as a "Saturday boy" in a local shop, where my work ethic certainly paid off. I progressed from being a part-time Saturday assistant to full-time assistant, deputy manager to store manager by the time I was 24 years old. My relationship with my family members was varied; from a dysfunctional relationship with my mother and a very close connection with my uncle. I spent wonderful days with my uncle on holidays, and in his work as a truck driver during my school breaks.

As a young adult, I was very conscious of doing the right thing and being respectful of other adults. My work in a retail environment and my responsibilities directly reflect this. When I was eighteen and old enough to visit pubs, I spent most of my evenings and weekends catching up with mates, playing pool and darts. This also became a frequent hook-up venue. Three relationships were formed at this pub, including with my first wife.

My first marriage broke down after our two children were born. This was due to my people-pleasing, deferring to others' needs for a quiet life, and my head-down-bum-up behaviour. This led to my wife having a relationship and child with another man. The situation created many occasions when I was confronted with this man, who was strong and forceful and who made physical threats with a loud voice. I had a few verbal encounters with him, his physical posturing and chest pumped out. I tend to become very withdrawn around this type of behaviour.

My second marriage was with a woman that I met through a brilliant life choice, when becoming involved with meditation and the Buddhist faith, which is still the essence of how I lead my life. We met at the local meditation centre and soon realised that we lived in the same street but had never met. A wonderful example of Karma in action.

In 2003, during this relationship, I was involved in a serious life and death accident as a pedestrian. This changed the direction of my life then and to the current day. My second marriage ended when my wife fulfilled her wish to become an ordained Buddhist nun, with my blessings.

Then karma played another huge part in my journey. I met an Australian woman, fell in love, and emigrated to Australia. We had a daughter, who is a massive part of my life. Unfortunately, my behaviour, which was exacerbated by the physical injuries and traumatic brain injury sustained in 2003, led me to using verbal, emotional and physical violence during the marriage, which ultimately led to its breakdown. We remain separated, but co-parent as effectively as we can.

I used to be very snappy at times. I used inappropriate and abusive language and was even physical at times, hitting my wife and pushing her roughly. I eventually searched out the Men's Behaviour Change Program as I accepted that there was a deep-rooted issue that I knew I needed to proactively learn about and action. If I didn't rectify my behaviour, it could cause catastrophic results for me, my wife and subsequently my young daughter in her ongoing development in relationships with others and her choices of male friends, partners and a father for her children. Nowadays I have become more aware of my actions and triggers, and of my physical pain and tiredness. I use techniques that I have learned during my journey.

I chose to join the local twenty-week Men's Behaviour Change Program. On my first night I was disappointed that my life choices had brought me to this. However, I was also incredibly proud that I had voluntarily joined the program. This showed that I still had enough self-awareness and self-esteem to see my own potential. I was quite daunted to walk into the group, not really knowing what to expect but knowing that there could be very strong characters that had also made bad choices that resulted in their being mandated to attend. I admit to feeling somewhat vulnerable.

I learned many things during the Men's Behaviour Change Program. The first was that family violence comes in many forms, many of which I did not associate with family violence. Most other men felt the same. Physical violence is obvious, but it can also include emotional, sexual, psychological, spiritual, verbal, cultural, cyber and financial violence. By the end of the twenty weeks of Men's Behaviour Change Program I personally noted and felt that although I had moved on in my self-awareness, I had merely scratched the surface. There was a great deal more to learn and develop.

I learned about a great number of topics, which unfortunately couldn't be looked at in detail due to the time restraints of a twenty-week program. I learned the names and principles. A few resonated in me more than others.

Two that impacted me significantly were the cycle of violence and the 5 x 5 rule.

The cycle of violence is a pattern of behaviour that, once described, was recognised in some form at least by most of the men present. It functions to keep survivors and perpetrators locked in the abusive relationship. Examining the cycle provided an understanding of its stages and how one could break the cycle at any chosen point. The cycle shows the stages of explosion or some form of violence or abuse and moves to remorse or guilt, promises that it will not happen again, and buy-back of the partner's affections and trust. This is often followed by a honeymoon phase and then the tension starts as the partner walks on eggshells, watching the escalation of anger until the violence happens again. And so the cycle continues.

It was very useful exploring what each partner might have been feeling at each stage of the cycle. I learned a lot from it as it reflected much of my behaviour. Most of all, it helped me understand what my wife and daughter were probably going through at the same time.

The 5 x 5 rule requires, most importantly, the ability to stop and think, probably the hardest thing we need to do. If we can stop and think, then we can change our thinking. One suggestion is that we ask ourselves the question, "Will it matter in five minutes, five hours, five days, five months, five years?" In other words, put the current situation in perspective and decide what attention, if any, it needs from you. This exercise has been very useful for me.

The opportunity to further expand my thinking and self awareness came with the second group I joined, which was ongoing. The first year or so allowed me to show up as a man able to positively and directly influence and be influenced by good male role models. The facilitators are responsible for leading the topics being discussed, but it's down to the men involved to actively participate and hold each other to account in respect of our own behaviours. I was prepared to support or even challenge other men appropriately, but was also able to appreciate challenges and constructive feedback, which helped keep me on track.

The group also allows men to have a check-in regarding any anger they experienced during the recent week between meetings. This could be due to being triggered by a partner, or indeed anyone in their life, or it could be an old behavioural issue that still needs to be worked on. This check-in enables men to vocalise in a helpful manner something that has troubled them but that they cannot see their way around. Other men learn as much from the check-in as the man sharing it, with insights being offered, confrontations and challenges made and empathy being created and felt by everyone.

The intense nature and depth of the group helps every man learn at his own pace. If an additional need is evident, the topic is extended by the facilitators, actively helped by other men who have a greater grasp of the topic from their personal experience. The topic that gets paused in one group meeting is taken up again at the next group meeting. This results in more growth for every man. The discussions get us closer to our wish to become the best man that we can, for ourselves and our relationships with partners and children.

My own self-esteem has been very low since 2003 and I have had to re-learn my role as a man, partner, husband and father in the world. But due to my active role in group and with the help of the other men as positive role models, plus the incredible support and encouragement of the facilitators, my self-esteem is markedly improved. My abusive behaviour is now replaced by a calm and focused determination to be the best man that I can be, for myself, my daughter and any future relationship.

Becoming involved in the group due to my poor behaviour and taking on the wisdom gleaned from other men's stories continues to inspire me to work with 'Men's Health and Growth', a program that connects me with millions of men across the globe.

I still delight in seeing my daughter two to three times a week. I am on polite terms with her mother and we try to set a good example as role models to our daughter and show that even though we are separated, we can still support each other."

Margaret says ...

Pete's first learning, which was accompanied by significant surprise, was the definition of family violence as presented to the group. As Pete says, this is not unusual. Most men and many women are unaware that the definition encompasses all that Pete has mentioned, as well as behaviour that is proactively neglectful. When men are made aware of it, they are usually horrified, as it highlights more of their behaviour that may be considered violent or abusive. Coming to group for the first time and finding that your behaviour may be even worse than you thought is a frightful thing. Pete had the courage to stay.

Denial is a common reaction at the start of the course, followed frequently by confusion and usually by an eventual understanding that their behaviour is unacceptable. By recognising and openly acknowledging their specific behaviour and its unacceptability, men are then able to take responsibility for their actions, which is the first critical step towards change. When this first happens to a group participant, I experience a great feeling of pride in the man's courage and relief that we can now move forward with the first steps of change. It is an extraordinary moment of honesty and vulnerability, but one without which no progress can be made.

If you are reflecting on past behaviour or contemplating behaving in a certain way, the question "Is it helpful?" will give you an answer that can guide your actions. If the answer is no, then clearly the action needs to be reconsidered and either omitted or changed to one that would not be harmful.

However, the "Is it helpful?" question, like the 5 x 5 rule Pete uses, depends upon stopping to think or, as I call it, "thought stopping". It's about making a conscious decision to change the music that is currently playing. This involves recognising that the current music is not to your liking and stopping it. But you must turn off the current music first. It's a conscious choice. The challenge for a man whose anger is escalating lies in the "thought stopping", that is, first changing the playlist. It can be so hard to do.

Many men's experience was that the time from trigger to physical violence or abuse was a matter of seconds, so there is little time for thought stopping. Identifying each man's triggers was an important part of the change process. A trigger is the "red button" or "hot spot" that a man chooses to react violently to. It's a big step to acknowledge that our triggers are in fact chosen by us and once we have identified them, they can be discarded. If the trigger receives the reaction of escalating anger, then thought stopping is needed in order to avert actions that cause hurt and pain.

When thought stopping is achieved, men find different ways of calming themselves. Some choose to meditate, others take time out, walk or run, count to twenty, put soothing music on, talk to someone they trust, have a rest, take deep breaths, consider the 5 x 5 rule which Pete finds useful, or put themselves in the shoes of the other person and consider what they may be feeling. If the chosen strategy distracts them from their escalating anger and hurts no one, then it is useful. If it increases self-awareness or makes someone else feel good, then it is particularly valuable.

Taking responsibility for his behaviour was not a new practice for Pete, who had adopted this course from an early age. When alone and unsupported in his distress he chose to succeed, despite the bullying and work overload he was experiencing. He turned his potential "I will be a victim" policy into goal-oriented determination and hard work – and he succeeded.

Pete acknowledges that the possibility of returning to abusive behaviour is ever present. His honesty is to his credit as there are never guarantees for either those who have been violent or abusive or those who have not, but he continues to work on his new self.

11

STEVE

"It's not what happens to you but how you react (respond) to it that matters." – Epictetus

Steve's story grew out of both face-to-face and phone discussions. He reworked some sentences and added little explanatory details until he was happy that his story accurately reflected the events in his life.

"I was always trying to find my place in the world and trying to sort out who I was," Steve said. "My parents always told me I was 'wild' and 'a handful'. They thought the way to manage me was through corporal punishment."

While a baby, Steve's family immigrated to Australia. He grew up in a strict Greek Orthodox family with two older brothers. Throughout his youth, he struggled to find himself between two often opposing cultures.

He tells his story here.

"My family was very patriarchal with Dad clearly king of the family. His word was law and, although he rarely hit me, the look on his face would tell me all I needed to know. We were all guided by the look on Dad's face.

Mum was the nurturing one, but even she would know how to generate shame. When frustrated, she would hit us at times with her slipper.

Overall, my parents were hard-working immigrants who had a very strong sense of what was right and wrong and who gave us many opportunities in life.

I was not close to my brothers. They had very different personalities to mine and seemed able to accept life with more equanimity than I could ever muster.

I managed primary school well enough and retain to this day a couple of my childhood friends.

Secondary school went well too. I managed to put in just enough work to pass Year 12 without unnecessary or excessive diligence. I also had enough skill to enjoy footy and soccer and make friendships that have lasted for many years. After school I went straight into helping Dad in his scallop fishing business until the business closed when the government banned fishing in Port Philip Bay. Dad was very ill at the time, so the impact of the closure was reduced by his health concerns. For me the closure meant the broadening of possible career options.

My dad and I unfortunately had one trait in common and that was a very short fuse which could explode into violence, leaping instantly from zero to a hundred on a scale that ignored all the numbers in between. I remember once when Dad exploded. He hit me hard across the face twice, leaving me very hurt and angrily nursing two bleeding nostrils. It took about three years for me to slowly thaw out and return to a reasonable relationship with him.

I also exploded with friends and family members, leaving me feeling either guilty or relieved to get things off my chest. I didn't know how else to express myself.

I often wondered if I learned this behaviour from Dad or inherited the trait genetically. However, no matter how I got it, I do know that it was a trait that was very hard to discard no matter what common sense told me should happen.

After the closure of Dad's business, a friend introduced me to the corporate world and there I moved through different facets of this world to management, in which I still work.

When I was 21, Dad died. His illness for two years prior to his death had prepared me. Much grieving had occurred during that time. I knew when the end came that it was time for Dad to go as the quality of his life was so diminished. I was then forced to step out of Dad's shadow and become more responsible and more independent.

I had a couple of girlfriends and a long-term relationship, which I see far more clearly in retrospect and about which I have felt great shame for my abusive behaviour at the time.

I was very controlling and given we were from different cultures and nurtured different goals, there was much to disagree about. I would become enraged and yell violent, abusive put-downs. At times I would throw things and although they were not directed at my partner, they would have been very frightening to witness. I expected to be the boss – after all, I was a man – and I **always** expected to have the last say.

Later, I met and married Susan, who is now my ex-wife. With the a similar Mediterranean culture, we did share common values. However, with Susan's depression and my undiagnosed ADHD to fuel friction, my abusive behaviour began again. At first it was occasional abuse amidst spans of honeymoon time together, but with the birth of two babies the honeymoon periods dwindled dramatically, and the fighting and my abuse escalated. The only physical violence occurred one day when I hit her on the arm. However, my behaviour was intimidating and abusive.

My eventual diagnosis of ADHD was no surprise to me. It just reinforced what I expected and put a label on me. That led to some treatment which helped somewhat. I love both my daughters very much, but it was my older daughter, who was about five years old at the time I was abusing Susan, who bore the brunt of my temper and my ignorance. I saw traces of me in her and since she was diagnosed with ADHD and had a temper something like mine, she was a challenge to control. I thought I would knock it out of her, and I carried out what I thought was discipline. I smacked her butt and held her by the neck under her chin as I yelled at her in anger and smacked her in the forehead. This was when the penny dropped – when I realised as I looked at her face that I had gone too far. She looked afraid and shocked.

Susan was also upset with me and wrote me a letter which spelled out her loneliness in the marriage as even when I was at home, I was not present. She was right. Work was stressful at the time and although I was physically at home, my mind was on my work. I went to join a Men's Behaviour Change Program, as recommended by a fellow with whom I played golf.

I confess I attended to appease my wife. I was still lacking awareness of the extent of the abuse I was dealing out and its impact on my family. Besides, I told myself that the other men were criminals and I was not like them.

It took weeks, but eventually with an increased understanding of what family violence was and its impact on others, I realised I was in the right place at the right time. I also realised that despite all the awareness in the world, much more was required to make changes that I could sustain in the future.

Life was up and down for some time. The children became used to trial separations. My behaviour remained abusive and threatening as I shouted, kicked doors and threw the phone on the floor.

One day I smashed my fist onto the car windscreen, cracking it as I did so. This was the last straw for Susan. She asked for another separation, during which time I stayed with my mother. Susan and I didn't reunite as we had in the past. A month later I was shocked to find Susan seeking legal advice about the splitting of our assets.

Soon after, Susan told me that the girls wanted to see me, so I took some work over to spend time there. Unfortunately, this finished in a loud, abusive altercation in which we wrestled over the phone and Susan ran from the house falling over and crying. My daughter and I helped her into the house before I went home. The neighbours must have called the police, because the police visited. I was issued with a safety notice preceding a court appearance a week later and the issuing of a family violence intervention order, to which I consented without admission. The order stipulated that the only contact I was to have with Susan was to be in relation to access to the girls. No photos of the girls were to be taken and no violence was to be perpetrated.

During this time, I completed the twenty-week Men's Behaviour Change Program and went on to join the follow-up program, which has higher expectations of its members and helps sustain and promote change. It was good to be among men who were motivated to maintain changes they had made and learn more about how they could become better men.

Meanwhile, I breached the intervention order conditions on two occasions, both of them by breaking the contact rules of the order. I was denied access to the girls for six very long months and put on bail. Access fortunately resumed. All went well until some months later when I breached the order again by discussing with Susan matters that were forbidden.

The police clearly decided to teach me a lesson – and teach me a lesson they did. They came to my home and, in front of my mother, they handcuffed me and took me away. My shame and my sorrow for my mother were enormous.

I was placed in remand alongside all sorts of criminals for six weeks, a time which felt like two years. I just couldn't believe this was happening to me. Above all, I was terrified that I would never see my children again.

I was shocked and fearful. That period made me appreciate what I had, and that never again would I take so much for granted. My release brought me the joy of space, taste and liberation, among much more. However, my mind was absorbed with trying to determine how to get access to my girls again. I missed them so much.

When I came out of remand it was like starting life over. I had resigned from my job, so finding any sort of work was essential. Getting access to my girls was top priority. It was during that time that I first discovered stoicism. I picked up a book which resonated with me: *The Daily Stoic: 365 Meditations on Wisdom, Perseverance, and the Art of Living* by Ryan Holiday. In a nutshell, I learned that it is not what happens to you in life but how you deal with it that matters.

This kept me from going to dark places when I walked endless kilometres thinking about my life, the choices I had made and, most importantly, when or if I would see my girls again. It helped me to maintain focus and patience, to deal with conflict, and to persevere through difficult times.

I got a job as a store person, and it took four-and-a-half months to get to see my girls again. It seemed like an eternity. It was my greatest purpose in life, and it eventually happened. My youngest daughter had no memory of the past abusive environment and came to me willingly. My older daughter took five minutes of uncertainty before resuming our relationship as before. I was able to apologise to her and before long she was demonstrating her latest karate moves.

I had to write to the group facilitators and explain why I thought I should be readmitted to the group. Men in this group were usually considered unsuitable if they perpetrated abuse or broke the law in any way. Fortunately, I was allowed to return.

The group also talked about the choice between reacting and responding to life's happenings and how you need to stop whatever you are thinking and make a conscious choice about whether you react spontaneously or whether you respond following consideration of the impact of your response.

Discovering just what family violence and abuse is and the impact it has on women and children was a very useful step for me, as was understanding the difference between discipline and punishment and the role teaching can play in the discipline of children. The 5 x 5 rule was a useful tool too, as it made me stop and think, which I knew was the first step to changing behaviour.

Perhaps one of the greatest influences on my change process was being part of a brotherhood of men with the same goals, the courage to be honest, empathy when I was down, and the capacity to make me feel a part of a team of men who were working together to become better people.

My parenting has improved greatly. I still raise my voice, but not in a threatening manner and I rarely lose my temper. My oldest daughter's behaviour can still be a challenge at times, but I try to manage her more calmly now and she is no longer frightened of me. However, she has a strong personality, and we still clash at times. I realise I am still a work in progress. I take comfort from advice a facilitator gave us: "You need to learn to live with discomfort".

The hardest thing for me to change was needing to always have the last word. There are times when I still find that a challenge, but usually I can stop and think and let the words on the tip of my tongue disappear. I tell myself that I can't change the past, but I can change the future.

Most importantly, my relationship with the girls has never been better. I have found a new partner who is calm and balances me out, and the girls respect and love her too."

Margaret says ...

Steve's description of his anger flaring up and "leaping" immediately from one to a hundred is shared by many men. A volcano undergoes myriad chemical and geological changes beneath the surface before it erupts. Scientists have learned to interpret and predict much of this activity over time. People are not volcanoes, but they do have many of thoughts and feelings hidden deep down, which fuel their anger.

Sometimes when a trigger has set of an escalation of anger, the speed of the eruption makes it difficult to identify the thoughts and feelings below it and to understand the role they play in the behaviour that is causing pain to others.

The trigger can be difficult to identify, particularly if it lies below a bundle of life's debris and takes some determined excavation to uncover. Untangling this assortment of thoughts and feelings is one of the hardest task men need to undertake. It may require a return to painful memories, and it certainly requires much courage and determination.

A major challenge for many men lies also in distinguishing between thoughts and feelings and determining the impact each has on the other. Feelings such as 'vulnerable', 'lonely', 'unloved', 'unlovable', and 'frightened' can be hard to admit to but necessary to confront when trying to unravel the turmoil deep below the surface of an explosion. Facing their feelings is vital if men want to find a way to prevent it from happening again.

Steve's openness to exploring himself and taking responsibility for his behaviour was brought about by his painful discovery that the law deemed him violent and abusive and that his behaviour was unlawful. Once he realised and accepted this, Steve was able to explore new ways of behaving and put into practice some ways of parenting his children that were loving and constructive, as well as ways of communication that positively impacted his future relationships. He was also able to support other men in the group by helping them appreciate the value of being in a group committed to the change process.

Steve was the man who first coined the term 'brotherhood' as a description of the group, the word carrying with it all the connotations of trust, honesty, and togetherness.

There is no doubt that for many men this 'brotherhood' environment was conducive to changes that may not have been possible otherwise.

12

MARCUS

"God grant me the serenity to accept the things I cannot change, the courage to change the things I can and the wisdom to know the difference."
– Reinhold Niebuhr

Marcus had the good fortune to spend a lot of his younger years with his "Nana", whom he loved dearly and still misses greatly. From the age of three Marcus would visit and stay overnight or spend weekends at his nan's house, partly to fill the void left by his grandfather's death and partly to give his pregnant mum a rest. His Poppa died when he was three, at the same time his mother was pregnant with his sister. Nana and Marcus formed a very strong bond. Nana was very caring and supportive of Marcus and this loving relationship continued into his twenties as they enjoyed spending time together and sharing gardening or other household chores.

Marcus's relationship with his parents was good, although his dad drank a lot. He would come home late at night and verbally abuse his wife. Marcus remembers him holding her against a wall once, but there was no other physical violence. However, despite this abuse, his relationship with both parents remained strong. Nana would praise him, pay him compliments, buy him chocolate treats and take him to lunch at the local coffee shop. She never had to berate him. He slept in her bed until he was twelve, which felt like the most natural thing in the world to him.

Nana smoked heavily, as had her husband. One day Marcus said to her, "Nan I don't want you to smoke any more" and she stopped smoking completely. This was a very special relationship.

Marcus was the firstborn in his family, followed by a sister three years later. After his parents' marriage broke up, his family expanded to include a stepdad and three stepsisters, and a half-sister born to his dad's second wife. Marcus's relationship with his father dwindled to occasional contact as his father became immersed in his new family. Marcus was at a bit of a loss. He was disappointed that his father took little interest in his sports and hobbies. He was never included in holidays with his father. An altercation at his dad's seventieth birthday ended in Marcus and his sister cutting ties with their father. Despite this, Marcus's partner offered his father the opportunity to visit and have a photo taken with his one-year-old grandson. The offer was declined. Marcus eventually grew to accept the reality of his changing world.

He and his sister were always included by their stepfather, who was a man of high integrity and who ensured all the children were treated equally. They enjoyed regular holidays together.

The time Marcus spent at primary school was happy. At the age of twelve he started part-time work at a petrol station, where he made friends with a family. One of them would later play a significant role in his life. He spent most of his weekends with these young men, which also contributed to him spending little time with his stepfather or father.

Secondary school presented a few challenges. In retrospect, he thinks he was at the wrong school. It particularly focused on academic achievement and music, whereas Marcus was a hands-on boy who liked nothing better than getting an uncooperative car going. He didn't belong to either of the two dominant groups, the nerds or the tough guys, and was subsequently bullied. He left school at the end of Year 10 and took up a motor mechanic apprenticeship.

After completing this he became a master mechanic and at the age of twenty-six was offered a job in the UK, where he lived for the next fifteen years. Although he visited home several times over that period, Marcus was saddened to speak to his Nana from England as she lay on her deathbed, imploring her to hang on as he would come to see her immediately. She died the next day. He was devastated. Another grandparent had died the year before, so Marcus decided to return home to Australia. He was missing his family and wanted to watch his nephews and nieces grow up.

Coming home was much harder than Marcus expected. He had built his own business in the UK and he didn't realise how much he would miss his customers, colleagues and the only real friends he had made as an adult. He felt lost. After several relationships Marcus, now aged 43, met Josie. Their relationship developed quickly. Marcus now believes that this was due not to Josie falling in love with him, but due to her need for security for her and her daughters and his support through the problems she was experiencing with her country of origin community. He believes she developed a fondness for him in time, as her girls became attached and called him Daddy.

From the first year of living together, life was chaotic. Josie's ex-partner was taunting her with religious and racial abuse despite an intervention order designed to keep him away from her. Marcus worked full-time, Josie couldn't drive, and was suffering mental health problems associated with a tumultuous childhood in the developing country from which she had migrated. They were forced to move house three times in three years. There were also two little girls requiring love and care.

Both Josie and Marcus were constantly stressed and over-whelmed by what was happening in their lives. On top of this, Josie was determined to realise her dream. They raised money to enable Josie to return to her homeland to visit her brothers and the graves of her parents. She left the children in Marcus's care for two weeks and on her return stated that she was the happiest she had ever been.

Josie became pregnant. She was diagnosed with cancer and five months after the birth of her son she had a hysterectomy and suffered early onset menopause while also experiencing postnatal depression.

Marcus took up his childhood friend's offer to try drugs to help him cope with a life that he found almost impossible to manage. He felt under great pressure to perform and carry out all the tasks associated with keeping a family healthy and happy. The drugs helped, but he soon realised that to keep them working he had to take more and his dependence grew. He did not take them socially but in private to boost his energy and keep his motor running.

Marcus agrees that this does not excuse his drug taking, which he deeply regrets and which he came to realise resulted in him detaching from family responsibilities when under the influence. He describes himself as an "absent parent" during that time, "not present" for the children as his mind was always focused on procuring more drugs to maintain his addiction. Marcus knew that Josie was opposed to drugs and struggled with the lifestyle that resulted from Marcus's addiction. The relationship was never perfect. They would have noisy discussions at times, but there was never violence. Abuse took the form of loud arguments, some of which were observed or overheard by the children who Marcus said "must have been scared".

When Josie left him, Marcus harassed and harangued Josie, both verbally and by text. Josie had disappeared with the children one day without explanation. It turned out she had told her case worker that she had been hit on one occasion, an allegation which Marcus denied then and now, and that Marcus was using drugs, an allegation that he did not deny.

Marcus was frantic until the police informed him the next day that she had taken out an intervention order against him. He was shocked, but turned up to court only to find that it would be adjourned for five months as neither Josie nor the relevant police officer was present. This meant that he couldn't see the children for five months despite the fact that no hearing had been held to determine his suitability to parent. Distraught, Marcus pleaded to be allowed to speak to the judge and at quarter past four was given a few minutes in court. He argued that there was nothing on the intervention order that suggested that the children were at risk from him. The judge agreed, removed their names from the order and wished Marcus luck.

Greatly relieved, Marcus tried to plan access visits. But despite the court order, the case worker refused to allow access. Josie contrived for Marcus to spend time with the children anyway. At no stage was he ever accused of poor parenting or inappropriate care of the children.

Marcus came to the Men's Behaviour Change Program voluntarily because although he hadn't been violent, he had been abusive and neglectful and he had an infant son and two little girls who were not his, but whom he loved dearly and wanted to care for. His access to his son was the matter proceeding in the Family Court at the time. The Family Court barrister recommended he join the program, so he did so immediately. Some weeks later, the court ordered him to do so based on the allegation that he had been violent. He had a positive outcome at court and was absolutely thrilled.

At first, Marcus was not too sure he was in the right place in the program, but within a few weeks he recognised how useful the group could be. It not only educated him, but also gave him skills to use in everyday life, particularly communication skills. Marcus didn't have to acknowledge and take responsibility for physical violence, but his drug use and the neglect, arguments and harassment that emanated from this took its toll.

The facilitators took him aside one evening and discussed with him what they assumed was his denial. They suggested that unless he cooperated by owning his problematic behaviour he may be asked to leave the group. Marcus was quite distraught by this – to the point of feeling suicidal. Being asked to leave the group would go against him in court. Above all, he wanted his son back, and the girls too if possible. He remonstrated with the facilitators, who allowed him to stay. He then joined the voluntary support group for men wanting to sustain change and learn more, and he continues this work until now, some eighteen months later at the time of writing this.

Josie returned to live with Marcus, but after she left again unannounced a voluntary agreement was made between Josie, Marcus and Child Protection regarding access. But instead, Josie took out a second intervention order. This made further allegations of breaching the first intervention order and alleged harassment by Marcus as he had repeatedly called her on the day she left the house and sent many text messages. Marcus turned up alone at court, and subsequent phone calls from the court to Josie resulted in her withdrawing the order. Josie admitted that she couldn't cope with the children on her own. An arrangement that suited all parties was agreed upon. Josie and Marcus have now demonstrated capacity to co-parent effectively for over a year.

Marcus has also remained drug-free for three years. He said, "I never, ever wanted to be a part-time parent, but I'm making the most of what I've got". I asked Marcus If he thought Josie would be prepared to write a few words or ring me. She called me and happily provided the following information after reading this story.

She said that Marcus is a naturally caring man who has changed a lot, particularly since he stopped using drugs. Now, she says, Marcus is very alert to her needs, communicates better and is more actively involved in the lives of the children because he is more present to them. He can reflect on the past and learn from it, and has become more stable and mature. The children, both Marcus's son and Josie's two children, are delighted to see Marcus when he picks them up and they clearly enjoy their time with him. Josie said she was glad this book was being written as she believes that people can change their behaviour and Marcus has demonstrated this.

Margaret says ...

This story exemplifies how neglect must be acknowledged as constituting abuse and how some complicated legal processes can affect all family members. Marcus was not innocent of any abuse, however he was confronted by challenges that threatened the relationships that mattered most to him: his children.

More importantly, what about the children? One must question the effect of all the comings and goings on them. How under-resourced must a court system be if children have to be separated from a parent for months before establishing whether such a separation is even necessary?

Marcus saw himself as a victim and he shed many a tear in the group, but he hung in there determined at least to become a part-time parent of his son and the girls if they wanted that. The girls did choose to come to him as a part-time parent, their relationship with their biological father no longer permitted by court order.

Attending the group helped Marcus climb out of the victim hole and respond to the ups and downs of life with greater composure, self-awareness and improved communication skills. Although extremely upset by the challenge from facilitators, he remained calm and continued at group meetings, as well as moving into another group at the conclusion of the first. He gave up the drugs after a couple of relapses and has been drug-free for three years at the time of writing this.

Challenging group members is a normal part of the group process. Men are encouraged to face up to challenges and even to challenge others in an appropriate way. Marcus thinks he is now a lot more considered in his responses, more able to consciously choose his battles and less likely to stress about those things that are out of his control. Perhaps some of the wisdom referred to in the quote at the start of this story has rubbed off on him.

Marcus's story also highlights the significant impact grandparents can have on the lives of their grandchildren. Other men have talked about the role grandparents have played or not played. Marcus appreciates the good fortune he had in enjoying such a loving, secure relationship with one grandparent in particular. Most of all, Marcus learned the hard way what we must all face. Our challenge in life is to manage what is sent our way to the best of our ability without harming ourselves or anyone else in the process. That is what the group is about.

13

———

VIKING

"From little things, big things grow." – Kev Carmody

When I think back on my childhood in Scandinavia, my thoughts are powerful and almost all positive. I recall an amazing relationship with my parents and my grandparents. We shared many activities together, particularly outdoors, and fishing and walking were two of our most popular pastimes. We were not what anyone would call rich, but we were comfortable enough.

I was very close to my mum. She was the most incredibly loving mum who would never fail to say "I love you" at bedtime, even if my younger brother and I had been naughty. She would often say "I will always be there for you. I will love you forever". Her love was unconditional and very protective. Dad loved us too, but he did not manifest it as passionately as Mum did. Still, we knew Dad loved us.

I picked up at an early age that Mum had emotional issues stemming from her abandonment by both her parents as a child. She was subsequently raised by her grandparents on an isolated farm in

Australia. One of my earliest memories was the arrival of an ambulance when I was four years old. Mum was taken to hospital following attempted suicide. Dad's explanation was that Mum was very sad.

Given that this theme wove through all my childhood and teenage years, I felt I had to become far more emotionally mature than was reasonable for my age. Although I remember a very happy life, it was certainly clouded with fear and uncertainty about Mum's welfare.

When I was six years old and my brother four, we came from Scandinavia to Australia to live, given my parents' expectation of a better life here for us boys. My grandparents were shattered and although we spoke on the phone on occasions, I, very sadly, never saw grandpa again. I would dream of them and cry in bed at night. I missed them so much.

We lived a similar outdoor lifestyle as we had in Scandinavia and Mum and Dad brought with them the Scandinavian philosophy of life that Mum loved so much. For my brother Jim and me that meant that we were never subject to corporal punishment or violence of any kind. Intolerance of any form of violence was ingrained in Scandinavian culture. In Australia, when Mum saw some children being smacked by their mothers in public, she was speechless. She couldn't believe her eyes.

The occasional arguments which we had witnessed between Mum and Dad became more frequent and more volatile. I was not of an age to understand why this was so. Dad was always subdued, but Mum became passionate and violent. She would be out of control, shouting, abusing, swearing, throwing things at Dad and at times threatening suicide with a knife taken from the kitchen before running outside.

I tended to mostly side with Mum as I could feel her pain, but she was very demanding of Dad, pressuring him to meet her emotional needs, which were great. I knew her expectations were somewhat unrealistic, but I felt for her.

We moved to a more isolated property in the country which

seemed to amplify Mum's problems. However, she was a very capable and determined physical worker, picking brussels sprouts for years. She was an intelligent woman, but her lack of confidence got in the way of her taking on any non-labouring type of work.

My closeness to Mum meant that I took on some of her way of managing life, including her means of dealing with conflict. It was like I took on the good, the bad and the ugly without realising the implications of doing so and the effect this may have later in life for me.

My schooling and sporting life went well. I continued through to Year 11. Life was good in so many ways, but my closeness to Mum resulted in my developing a morbid fear of something happening to her. I worried that she would finally kill herself after what had been many attempts. I worried that my friends would see her when she was out of control. Her unpredictability created the tension associated with living with uncertainty and I came to more fully realise that her excessive love, although totally genuine, was born out of compensation for what she grieved for in her childhood.

Mum did seek help, but nothing changed. She would always create dramas and had a habit, driven by insecurity and perhaps paranoia, of debriefing and analysing anyone that came into our lives. In retrospect, I can see that my constant exposure to Mum's behaviour as I experienced it meant that I took on the way in which she managed emotional issues and her tendency to over-analyse people.

Later in high school, when I was seventeen years old, I went fishing with a mate. Mum had dropped me off in a nearby town and I had ridden my bike, carrying a few beers, to the fishing spot.

We were sitting with our lines in the water when I noticed a police car drive over the nearby bridge and back. My suspicions grew as two police officers got out of the car and walked towards us. I knew I was about to hear something I didn't want to hear. Sure enough, once I had identified myself at their request, the police told me that there had been a car accident and Mum had died.

It was surreal and very difficult to describe, but something happened inside me at that moment which alerted me to the possibility that this would happen.

My first thoughts were for my brother, who was home alone on the farm. Dad was away in Scandinavia visiting my sick grandpa and when the police offered to contact Dad, I advised them that I would do so. My mate was in shock, but we went home to tell my brother Jim. I called Dad, who returned home as quickly as he could. Telling Dad was one of the hardest things I have ever done. They had been married twenty years and still loved one another.

I took on Mum's role and I guess I did everything she would have done. I played protector, bill payer, funeral organiser and supporter to Dad and Jim. Dad was a gentle man whom I loved. I knew he loved me too, but my relationship with Mum was very close, maybe even unhealthily so. I was enormously saddened by Mum's death, but despite this closeness – or maybe because of it – I confess with some discomfort to a slight sense of relief. She had been a tortured soul and now she was at peace. Dad and I need no longer live in fear and trepidation of what she might do next.

From that day on, although Dad was the breadwinner, I was the man of the house. I had no fear of my own mortality as nothing worse could possibly happen. I had lived through what I figured would be the hardest time of my life.

I chose the local Catholic priest to conduct the funeral service because although she was not actively involved in the church, Mum was Catholic. I had bumped into him on numerous occasions at school and footy and other communal activities. The funeral was a massive affair attended by hundreds of people, a group of whom formed a guard of honour for Mum. I was satisfied that we had farewelled her as well as we possibly could.

The priest became almost an extension of our family, so it felt weird and confusing the first time he sexually abused me at an overnight camp. I resisted, but didn't really pick up just how inappropriate his behaviour was until the second and third time when, although I pushed him away, I was overcome with a sense of great shame. I tried to put the incidents to the back of my mind and just get on with life. At the time I seemed to do so successfully.

Once I finished high school my ambitions to travel and visit Grandma, who had visited us once in Australia, came to fruition. I spent the next two-and-a-half years travelling most of Europe and Southeast Asia. I enjoyed great times with Grandma, which was fantastic for me and generally created what have turned out to be some of the most wonderful experiences of my life.

I fell in love easily and my general zest for life helped me forget some of the unfinished business I had left behind or hidden down deep, like grieving for Mum and the sexual abuse. It was, to some extent, a period of my life marked by an element of escapism.

I fell in love with a Swedish girl who terminated our pregnancy and our relationship, which upset me greatly, and so I held back somewhat when I was back in Melbourne and met Susan from the Wimmera. Despite my unresolved issues, this relationship slowly developed into one that lasted twelve years and to which our four beautiful children were born.

Early on, Susan's relationship with her mother became a little strained. I worried about it as I wanted a family that was happily connected. I was a bit pushy and controlling, wanting only the best for my family. Occasional angry outbursts from me became the norm. It never entered my head that this was the start of family violence and abuse. This was normal, I thought. In fact, our relationship was still fine. We were good friends for most of the time.

I got a job in a computer company, even though my knowledge and skills were insufficient. My boss was terrific and apart from one plunge into disfavour when I made a mistake concomitant with my lack of knowledge and he gave me a hard time, we remained friends even after I moved into a totally different field. He was my friend and mentor and he taught me much about life, for which I will always be grateful to him.

My occasional gambling and brief infidelities didn't really spoil the harmony of our family that I loved, as far as I could tell. I did, though, feel at times that I was modelling myself on Mum, especially when I became angry and verbally abusive. To my knowledge, verbal abuse was just part of family life and certainly did not come under the umbrella of family violence, but in retrospect I see that things were building up. This was a mixture of my early life experiences and what I saw as social expectations. I was thinking, "I'm not perfect, but I love my partner and kids and I'm being a good Dad and getting on well with everyone".

The time came when I felt the need to move on in my career. I decided that to move to the country town where Susan's parents lived and where they were well-known as it would be great for the family. I managed to get a job in a nearby town where I was primarily seen by other employees as an intruder, so I spent a fair bit of time alone, having a beer at the pub or placing bets.

However, one day the local pub was put on the market and my mind started racing. I discussed the matter with the publican, who said words that I've never forgotten.

He said, "There are three things that can really stuff you up, the punt, the piss and the pussy". In other words, you must go into this job with strong moral values and high integrity. So, aged twenty-eight, I became a publican. It was not all that I had expected it to be.

We lived in a part of the hotel that was a residence and, although there were many rooms to let, only one room was permanently occupied. The others were rarely in use. Nevertheless, business went quite well, and we never knocked back a sponsorship of a local team or a wedding as venues were hard to find for such events. We were very community minded. I believe we did quite a good job, though the hours were very long. I was never off duty. I also needed to develop a persona that was highly respected, and even a little bit feared, as security was an issue that I could be confronted with at any time. I stayed overnight in Melbourne every two or three weeks where I experimented a little with speed (methamphetamine). More escapism, I guess.

Unfortunately, I also gambled a couple of times, losing money we could ill-afford to lose. The second time I lost about twelve thousand dollars, which meant that the TAB facility was removed from our pub and I was charged by the police. I received a suspended sentence. Susan and I were extremely embarrassed by my behaviour, particularly as her family was so well-respected by the townsfolk.

It took time, but eventually I seemed to be forgiven and life returned to normal.

It was some twelve months later that disaster struck. After I had gone to bed around 1:30 am towards the end of a young man's twenty-first birthday party, I heard a slight scratching sound downstairs and then smelled something like electrical burning. The fire alarm went off.

I raced downstairs and saw smoke coming from the false ceiling near my office, which was situated almost underneath the stairs. I sent the birthday man and his family out to safety and, almost unable to breathe, I ran back upstairs, where my family was screaming and struggling to breathe as the smoke was so thick. It was like being underwater. I thought to myself, "so this is how it all ends". Somehow, Susan and I managed to get a child each under our arm and make our way to the balcony door, which I kicked in. We made it out on to the balcony as the stairway was too thick with smoke for us to descend.

The Country Fire Authority was not equipped to deal with such a blaze and their ladder did not reach us. We were trapped. We called for Susan's uncle, who owned a cherry picker. He finally arrived and plucked us from the balcony and deposited us on the ground. As I was about to leave the balcony after the rest of the family had been removed, I remembered the man who permanently occupied the end room of the corridor and ran down towards him, shouting his name. He stumbled out and we both rode the cherry picker to the ground where we stood on the street with the local CFA and other onlookers, struggling to regain our breath and thankful to be alive. We watched in horror as everything we had ever owned, every photo, every item, went up in flames. It was an indescribable experience that took us so close to death and was massive in its impact on the family and me.

The CFA started smashing windows to get their hoses in, which of course gave the fire more oxygen to fuel it, so I gave them the keys and they unlocked a door instead as we stood among TV cameras and watched. I agreed to a brief interview. I overheard the interviewer ask someone as he walked away, "Do you think he had anything to do with it?". I was incensed and I immediately remonstrated with him, shouting, "Pull your head in. My kids were nearly killed". I was devastated.

A detective from outside town came to interview me and I responded in what had become my normal confrontational manner in those days. I had adopted a demeanour of ruling with an iron fist. I eventually explained that not only did I have enormous love for my kids, but I was also very temporarily uninsured, as current financial and insurance transactions could attest to, so I had no motive to burn down the pub.

So much of you changes when something as big as this happens. I had been working as a publican, living as a father and a partner as best I could, but the ramifications of the event and the logistics of managing what was left of it took its toll on me.

It was devastating for all the family. The kids were resilient. It was tough to know how to address it, but the overwhelming emotion from all of us was relief, particularly from Susan. We understood the importance of love and family over materialistic things. We had got as close to death as you could. We literally thought we were going to die and had come close to passing out. However, the kids moved forward quickly as we didn't dwell on the event or show too much emotion in front of them.

It took months before forensic investigators allowed us to enter the building. Eventually we did and realised that everything had gone. We were financially ruined. I filed for bankruptcy.

The arson squad conducted further investigations and seemed to imply some guilt on my part by asking how come the door to the outside was open. I explained that I had given the key to the CFA to enable them access for their hoses, but the inference that I was under suspicion undid me. I went off my head and exploded, shouting at them that my family had nearly died. Another cop, seeing that I was about to become violent, ushered me into a cop car and calmed me down. A forensic investigator told me she thought the computer or modem had started the fire as that is the area where it had originated.

Although there were still some insinuations from one cop, the townsfolk were very good to us. We were flooded with food, clothes and money. It was fantastic and will never be forgotten.

My old boss and friend said that if I needed money, then I should move into the automotive industry, which I did with considerable success. It was a massive career move. I was absolutely horrified at the regimented sales process that was required, but it was at least legal. I had to earn money, so I went with it. We moved back to Melbourne, where we rented a house and my work progressed until I reached management level.

Meanwhile, my relationship with Susan was going downhill. It was my fault. I just couldn't settle again, much as I loved Susan and my children. I was just different. Within a year I had met Kim, and a new connection was established before the other had finished. I had sent the family back to the country town, as Susan's mother was very ill. I was lonely, but that is no excuse. To this day I deeply regret the hurt I caused Susan and the children. Telling Susan that we were finished became the hardest thing I've ever done.

I continued daily contact with the kids for a long time, but after another man came into their life, the children's interest in me dwindled. I live in hope that they will want to re-establish a relationship with me one day so that I can try to compensate for the pain and hurt I inflicted upon them.

Although Kim and I connected well, the relationship was doomed from the start. I was emotionally damaged. I wanted everything done my way, I needed to always be heard and I couldn't live with uncertainty, so control became my greatest need. I was also drinking and gambling.

After six years I arrived home one day to find all my possessions out on the footpath. It was over. I was so shocked. I couldn't believe that I was not in control. How could that be?

I lived alone for two years, during which I spent time examining myself and self-evaluating, learning to live with myself and generally maturing, I think. I believe in retrospect that it was good for me to be alone for a time.

I had numerous short-term relationships, the last of which was with Jenny. Both of us had experimented a little with recreational drugs and it was part of our relationship. Jenny informed me that she had been horrifically sexually abused from childhood to late teenage years and that she had eventually gone to the police to report the abuse. This set me thinking that I should report my experience of sexual abuse, so I went to the Melbourne Response to Clergy Abuse program and told my story.

Everything I said was recorded and my psych assessment diagnosed me as having severe post-traumatic stress disorder, PTSD. I was offered an entitlement and was required to sign a document which ensured confidentiality.

My relationship with Jenny fell apart. It was a horrible, tumultuous time. I went downhill from there. I was starting my own business in the racing industry and after coming out about my sexual abuse, my use of drugs increased. I discovered that the person I thought I was, and that I thought other people saw me as, had changed. I was no longer the "me" that I used to be.

Coming to grips with an understanding of PTSD led to me self-medicating with methamphetamine, which provided me with a dangerous but very subtle and very repeatable feeling of euphoria. It kept me going – or I should say I kept it going – and when I met Melinda this use of drugs was something we had in common.

We met through our mutual interest in horse racing and both of us were caught up in a web of deception regarding our drug use and our families. Melinda had a ten-year-old son of whom I took over fathering to a large extent. However, Melinda and I still both used drugs and our addictions affected our ability to carry out our work effectively.

We moved to three acres in the outer suburbs, which gave us the opportunity to purchase our first horse. Still, my emotional problems were there, and the usual verbal abuse took place as before.

To seek help for Melinda, I spoke to her parents, who became increasingly concerned about the whole situation. Melinda became pregnant and her fight to control her drug habit continued throughout the pregnancy. I became more and more abusive, yelling, hitting and slapping her and generally behaving in an extremely combative way. I became quite paranoid and thought I was being followed or that Melinda was trying to poison me. I would disappear for days at a time without a phone. Everyone was worried about me. I had lost the plot completely.

If I wanted drugs, I would wrestle the keys out of Melinda's hands and slap her. I had no tools with which to dig myself out of the hole I was in, so I would disappear in fear of what I would do if I stayed. I was out of control and at the peak of my family violence and abusive behaviour.

Gradually, I descended into a world of crime to get money to feed my addiction. This included car thefts from the airport and stealing jewellery from jewellers from whom I would run like the blazes with a ten-thousand-dollar gold chain in my hand.

Our lifestyle and my behaviour resulted in Melinda's son being taken to live with his father and our one-year-old daughter being taken by the Child Protection team of the DHS and placed with Melinda's parents. We were devastated, but still unable to put an end to our addictions.

We were meeting with a dealer in a city street when I lost my temper with Melinda and the police stepped in and arrested me. I was remanded in custody for six weeks. Never in my wildest dreams did I think I would end up in prison. I was shattered and my family was very concerned indeed. At the court hearing at the end of the six weeks, the judge read the psychological assessment that I had undergone and commented that for someone who had led a crime-free life, I had certainly made a spectacular entry into the criminal world. That was so true.

I was released on a community corrections order. I returned home, joined Melinda in the use of drugs again and lasted six weeks before being arrested once more, this time as I ran out of a jeweller's shop with stolen goods.

I was in prison for three months and when I was released again, I continued the same drug-fuelled lifestyle at the same time as fighting with Melinda to get our daughter back. We were allowed only half an hour a fortnight of access, and it was terrible. It certainly did nothing to motivate us to stop our drug use. It was a vicious cycle. Eventually we were both arrested. I received a three-year sentence reduced on appeal to sixteen months.

This time was different. The moment I stepped into my cell, I made a decision to never touch drugs again. I'd had a taste of what life could be like if drug-free and I wanted to get back to it, but I found I had to fight to get assistance in achieving that goal.

I decided the best way to start was by doing everything I could to help others. I threw myself into it and started the course required to become a peer educator, the highest-ranking position a prisoner could hold. A peer educator, once trained, became the prisoner available for others to talk to if they had a problem and didn't want to confide in a staff member. Hence it was important to also earn the respect of the men. Qualifications alone were not enough, but I completed all the necessary training.

I was in a division which housed the full gamut of criminals from homicide down, except for sexual offenders. Over my sixteen months I spoke with and listened to many men, some quite notorious, and I talked to groups of fifty to sixty prisoners at a time, telling them to make the most of this opportunity to turn their lives around.

My philosophy was that I had to walk the walk if I was to talk the talk. My personal goal was to turn my life around for the sake of myself as a human being and for Melinda and my children. I called it a "life renovation". I learned such a lot about human nature. I left prison this time with a desire to help others, but knowing that I had more work to do on myself first.

I was accommodated in a boarding house with nothing but the three hundred and fifty dollars that I had saved in prison. I was starting life again.

After returning to Melinda, I stated very clearly that I was no longer going to use drugs and that she could only come with me if she was prepared to do likewise. The alternative would mean the end of our relationship. Melinda came with me. She gave up the drugs and between us, both drug-free, we went to battle to have our daughter and Melinda's son returned to us. We were clean, we were free, and we were happy as we started our journey towards getting the kids back.

I had an amazing psychologist, as did Melinda, and we had amazing DHS workers and lawyers who did all they could to support our quest. The fight continued for eighteen months, through seven or eight hearings, and with three tests per week to prove our non-use of alcohol and drugs. We passed them all. We had access with our daughter for only one to two hours per fortnight and we would cry afterwards.

It was easier with Melinda's son. His father, who was caring for him, recognised the changes we were making and was supportive of us, although we still had two court appearances to get through before he could return to live with us.

I voluntarily joined the Men's Behaviour Change Program, thinking it was ridiculous to start with. But my view soon changed as I realised that this was life-changing stuff. I continued into the follow-up group, which was a unique group of men, all voluntarily seeking the same outcomes. Melinda would comment that I was different when I came home from group, somehow more buoyant and more comfortable with myself.

However, there is never a situation where you can go to a group or a course and come out saying that you have now changed. You can reduce cholesterol or lose weight, but with family violence you have to work on it daily like you do with drug or alcohol addictions, using the tools and skills you learned in group. This need not be a burden. It's more a matter of remaining mentally alert and self-aware. It's a bit like an alcoholic who, after twenty years of living alcohol-free, is still technically an alcoholic.

The group gives you peers who have not walked in your shoes, but who share some understanding of how you feel, have some empathy if you like. No comparisons are made, and no judgements given. We are accepted as we are and allowed the freedom to be our real selves. This is grounding and helps us build a solid foundation on which to create change.

I went to jail thinking men who committed violence and abuse or any other crime could not be rehabilitated. I was wrong. Change takes honesty, the capacity to acknowledge that you have a problem and the motivation to seek help and use it.

Life is about choices. When you are being violent and abusive, you have chosen to do so. I got away with so much, as do so many men who think they have some sort of entitlement to behave in certain harmful ways. Do I want my children to grow up like this? No, I certainly do not.

It takes years for other people to accept that the changes you have made are genuine. That often ongoing distrust is hard to bear, but liking yourself again makes it all worthwhile.

Margaret says …

Viking chose the quote that opens his story because he thought the words best illustrated his life. Although his interpretation of these lyrics differs from the writer's intention, it is equally valid. Throughout his life, Viking learned that when problems occur, they need to be dealt with at the time rather than letting them silently fester and magnify until they can no longer be contained and their eruption harms loved ones as well as oneself.

His story brings this home to the reader in no uncertain terms. The walls he built around various episodes and events in his life were strong and, he hoped, insurmountable, but they cracked under pressure, releasing years of unexamined emotion including grief, fear, shame and much more.

I imagine some of our readers, like Viking once did, do not believe men can change. One of the judges who awarded Viking and Melinda custody of the children again commented that she had never witnessed such an enormous change as Viking and Melinda had achieved.

Change simply requires one tiny but honest glimpse of ourselves as we really are, or as others experience us, and a mighty dose of motivation. From that tiny but honest moment of self-examination, big change can grow.

However, like some of the other men, Viking's lack of knowledge or understanding of what constituted family violence and abuse, combined in part with his denial, meant that it was years before he recognised it for what it was and that it needed to change. Self-examination needs to be accompanied by education, an understanding of what constitutes family violence and abuse and importantly, its impact on family members.

Viking mentioned that he thought that some men felt, either consciously or subconsciously, that they were entitled to behave in certain ways. This sense of entitlement, which many men – often with great reluctance – recognise in retrospect, is hard for them to acknowledge, as entitlement has grown up with them and has not been taken on board in a deliberate and conscious way.

While Viking claims that he benefited greatly from the group, it is fair to say that he had a lot to give. When he moved house to a location too far for him to attend the group, we were all disappointed, as with his breadth of life experience he contributed much to many men.

14

WRITTEN AND UNWRITTEN STORIES

"Self-control is strength. Calmness is mastery. You have to get to a point where your mood doesn't shift based on the insignificant actions of someone else. Don't allow others to control the direction of your life. Don't allow your emotions to overpower your intelligence." – Morgan Freeman

Aspects of your own behaviour over which you do not hold mastery may well become mastered by others. Some men chose not to write their stories for this book. Despite being very keen supporters of the group and positive influencers of other members, and despite having changed their abusive behaviour and sustained that change over several years, the time was not right for them to delve into their past. They agreed with the idea of this book, but for a range of reasons they were not yet ready to reveal their stories in writing.

Their reasons varied and, simple or complicated, I understood that the time was not right for them. The men are encouraged to see themselves as their own experts in the change process. Reliving the past could plague a storyteller, forcing him to question himself. Other life traumas beyond the abusive behaviour could get in the way of reopening history.

Fear could play a role in discouraging a man from returning to the past, fear of the impact on him and his family. Would they support him? Would it affect his most important relationships? Could he face those past life events without falling apart? Is the time right to do this? Readiness impacts all the decisions we make in life, and this was no different.

Some of the men have forgiven themselves for their past behaviour, but others have not, and will not, until such time as they can wield the pick and shovel and dig out the shame and hurt that is so deeply buried.

"It can be easier to put it all behind me," said one man, knowing that unfinished business does not always stay behind and can infiltrate the future.

For men who have perpetrated violence or abuse or made bad decisions which have nagged and reverberated over the years, taking responsibility for their behaviour and openly acknowledging it means courting shame. Men have described shame differently, but frequently it was said to look and feel like a dark, heavy, ugly rock that sits deep inside, relentlessly weighing down the person bearing it. At times, the weight of shame would hang in the group room like a morbid gloom. The group facilitators would try to finish the group on a positive note to relieve the men from carrying extra weight home with them. Otherwise the gloom of shame and pain could be contagious.

Shame can also be a motivator. It can be usefully employed to assist change, although some men say that it can be very hard to eradicate shame even when major changes have been made. The challenge lies in taking responsibility for violent and abusive behaviour and owning it, even when by doing so shame increases. Only then is it possible to feel pride in new, positive ways of behaving and forgive yourself as you move forward. The more pride you take in yourself, the easier it is to let go of the shame.

While shame and guilt are hard to carry, self-forgiveness is so important if long-term change is to be sustained. Maintaining confidence, assertiveness and other elements of balanced emotional maturity is difficult when shame lies unresolved, undermining and sabotaging the route forward. It nibbles constantly at confidence, strips assertiveness, and plays havoc with self-doubt.

Some months after their stories were completed, I asked the men how they felt when writing them and/or reading them when they were finished.

Although I told Thomas that I had found his story and insights particularly useful, he said that he had struggled to understand the relevance of writing his story, both for himself and the wider community. Thomas prefaced this with the comment that his feelings about the story were influenced by high anxiety and low confidence. However, I am hopeful that any readers who have ADHD or are closely associated with someone who has it will find Thomas's story helpful.

The other men hoped that telling their stories would be useful. They wanted not only to change themselves, but also to have some impact on changing society by reducing family violence of any kind. Although many men experienced vulnerability as they prepared for people to read their personal journeys, this was overcome by the hope that someone somewhere might find their story helpful.

One man said that writing his story illustrated clearly how much he had learned. He said he was able to say, "That's the sort of person I was and look at me now!"

He, along with others, described writing as a cathartic experience, clearing the way for more learning and giving confidence that more could be achieved to help men change their abusive behaviour.

Public ownership was seen as an important part of delivering their stories, and men felt pride in their capacity to expose themselves through their writing. One man said that reflecting on his past to write his story highlighted how much he had brought upon himself and how pleased he is with his progress from making poor choices to where he is now. He said, "I am so glad I changed".

Change can be brought about through different methods of learning or by unforeseen triggers. In many instances, the trigger that leads to seeking help for abusive behaviour is a crisis, often involving the police, the threat of incarceration or a family breakdown.

Sometimes a slow-creeping awareness that the man is not becoming the adult he wanted to be, or a sudden awakening to the fact that he has fallen short of his own expectations, leads him down the path of exploring what help is available.

Men who are mandated to attend Men's Behaviour Change Programs have no choice in how or whether they wish to approach the change challenge. If they had wanted to, they may not have chosen group work as their way to embrace change.

Those men who have made their own decision to explore the possibility of changing their behaviour have a choice. What sort of help would most benefit them?

Group work is certainly a good fit for many men, but individual face-to-face work may be more suitable for some. That may begin with a trusted friend or family member, counsellor, psychologist or psychiatrist.

For some men, browsing websites for videos of relevant talks may be a great starting point. A phone call to a crisis line can provide food for thought and options to consider. And for some men, finding a book that unexpectedly touches them in a way that provides clarity and generates motivation is progressive.

Mindfulness or meditation practices, either individually or in group sessions, are greatly valued by some men. This couples well with all other forms of help.

Whatever choice is made, the first step may be cautious, uncertain, or even fearful, a trial that carries no more commitment than one step. Motivation may be shaky until the man is convinced of his need to change and feels safe enough in an environment to commit to taking another one or more steps.

Many men, particularly those whose change process is complicated by mental health or addiction issues, may choose to combine two channels of assistance for greater effect. Usually, if a friend or family member is prepared to support a man in his change journey, then the way forward is likely to be a little smoother and less lonely for him.

All means of support and assistance are valid and each has its advantages. One aspect of group work that is not shared by other approaches is learning from other men. All men in groups, in my experience, would enthusiastically agree that learning from other men's personal experiences is greatly beneficial to positive outcomes.

Ultimately, whichever path is chosen, the men must show immense courage, as any learning and self-growth may easily be stunted if not accompanied by complete honesty – a confronting personal challenge. These men have met that challenge.

15

NEXT STEPS

These twelve men's stories have been told in the hope that doing so will make a difference. Some came to the program voluntarily to change their behaviour, while others were mandated by court orders. Together, they are a very small portion of the total. This book shows they are real people, not just faceless statistics. They have been humanised, which raises the fear for some people that these men are very adept at image management – which indeed many perpetrators are.

Humanising the men can also be seen as an opportunity to know the whole man and not just the part that behaved monstrously. We come to see the men's positive traits, which can be nurtured back into action to create and sustain changes in behaviour – provided the motivation and determination are there too.

I recall, many years ago, talking to the mother of a young man who had just been incarcerated for a particularly violent and gruesome murder. One of the first things she spoke of was her recollection of her son as a little boy with his small wheelbarrow, helping her in the garden. This man was certainly where he should be, but her anecdote illustrates that it is possible to find strengths and positive attributes in most people. The hard work begins when these attributes are unearthed and put to work to create change.

The history of most of the world is patriarchal, as it is here in Victoria, Australia. Women, and many men with us, continue to battle for equality in a range of spheres. The media has focused, rightly so, on the enormous toll on women from homicide and other violence and abuse. Much is being done to support and enable women and children to live safe, fear-free lives. More is still needed.

Something has been done to stop the behaviour of men who are causing this maelstrom of violence. These twenty-week courses are of really good value. Many men need more, and need longer. Some have to change years of violent behaviour and the origin of some behaviour is rooted in life events that occurred twenty, forty or sixty years ago. Twenty weeks, no matter how good, may not be long enough for them to change behaviour so deeply buried for so long.

Little is known about these courses outside of those conducting or participating in them. Research has yet to determine their value in changing men's behaviour long-term. However, researching the successful change in men after only twenty weeks may simply reflect that the course is nowhere near long enough.

Most men who have been violent or abusive never hear about groups like this unless they are mandated to attend, call a generic helpline, or hear from someone who has attended. Why are we not seeing more public messaging specifically directed towards men who want to change their behaviour. Many people believe that men cannot change their behaviour and that funding programs is a waste of taxpayers' money that should be put towards care of vulnerable and hurt women and children. Of course, this is understandable.

However, this book show that there are men who want to change their behaviour and they can do so. What better way to reduce the number of hurt women and children than by addressing the cause, buoyed by the knowledge that some men want to change? How many men are out there right now perpetrating violence or abuse without really understanding that their behaviour fits that definition, or is beginning to?

How many women are still unaware that their partner's behaviour comes under the banner of family violence and abuse? Advertising at least points them in the direction of help with statements like "If you or anyone you know is affected by abuse or violence call [number]". This is terrific, but why are we not seeing ads like "If you think you have been violent or abusive to any family members and want to change that behaviour call [number]. Help is available."

Over the past ten years and during the process of writing this book, the one thing that has consistently leaped out at me has been the men's need for education. Perhaps it is the whole community's need. The ignorance (and I say that kindly and with understanding of how this can come to be) is enormous. Men must take responsibility for their behaviour, but we cannot expect them to be responsible for their own education as children and young people, particularly when education happens in a range of environments – school, home, clubs, and from peers and role models. So many men have said that they wished they had this learning much earlier in their lives because if they had, their partners and children would not have been abused or affected by abuse. And they would not be carrying a lump of shame in their gut.

I don't think any man knew the full definition of family violence before attending Men's Behaviour Change Groups, let alone any ways to make the changes required to exchange their behaviour for something helpful. Underpin that with the fact that so many men are still raised with the expectation that real men don't cry and real men don't seek help on emotional issues and you have a recipe for the abuse of women and children.

We need to get into schools even more than we are now. Years 10, 11 and 12 would benefit greatly from a course specifically on this subject, and it would not be difficult to design one for teenage boys and girls. I am delighted to hear that courses relating to respect have begun in schools, as have gratitude, empathy and mindfulness courses been addressed. These are known as 'GEM' courses.

Girls would benefit from understanding what constitutes violence, abuse and coercive control, what their options are if they experience abuse, and above all the confidence that comes from understanding one's value and rights. Boys would benefit from knowing how violence and abuse is legally defined and what help is available to boys whose behaviour is moving that way. All would benefit from learning about conflict resolution and responding to disrespect.

Let's not wait until violence and abuse happen. Let's put the money into more education as a preventative measure. No, it would not stop all abuse, but it would certainly help.

Long-term support groups for men who have completed the Men's Behaviour Change Program are also needed. Twenty weeks is rarely long enough to change an entrenched pattern that has been recycling for many years. Most of the men whose stories are written here have completed the Men's Behaviour Change Program as well as three years of further group work.

One-off sessions could be designed for sporting clubs, with supports for further individual help if required. I understand that some of this already occurs.

The men in my last group have great skills and understanding of the issues. Let's use some of their newfound knowledge and skills. They now carry much wisdom. Let's share it around. They could certainly help in the design of a program that would be most likely to meet the needs of young people.

RETROSPECT IS A WONDERFUL TEACHER, but the downside is that so often the journey to retrospect is littered with pain, particularly the pain of women and children. Certainly we can learn from pain, both our own and that of others, but how much better it would be if the learning happened before the retrospective journey was needed.

The theme that seems to run consistently through these stories is ignorance – understandable and explainable, but there nevertheless. And buried feelings, deep pockets of shame and guilt. Ignorance seems to have been present at several different levels. Many of the men did not know that some of their behaviour constituted family violence. They all knew about physical violence, including sexual assault or rape, but there is of course so much more.

Imagine the discomfort of nervously attending the first session and then finding out that lesson number one gave you even more reason to dislike yourself. The guilt was increased and the shame magnified, consciously or subconsciously, as the facts sank in and the realisation came that society defined family violence far more broadly than they expected.

The men had little idea how to change their behaviour. Even getting to the point of adopting strategies and techniques to manage their behaviour was fraught, because it required them to recognise the abuse, acknowledge its presence in their lives, own their abusive behaviour and find the motivation to change it, all before they could gain any value from exploring ways to turn that behaviour around.

Most men had never heard of empathy before. Without empathy only superficial change is possible. Empathy provides the reason and hence the motivation for authentic change –authentic because it is directly motivated by an understanding of how their behaviour impacts others.

Many men had not heard of men's groups, including the Men's Behaviour Change Program, nor did they have any idea that a group that was non-judgemental despite being clear about what behaviour was and was not acceptable, was available.

Finally, many men did not know that there were people out there who not only believed they could change, but who would support them as they tried to do so.

If all this "knowing" was accessible, or "unavoidable learning", when these men were teenagers, what different stories may be told.

And if we add to that education for young men and women about parenting and the impacts of violence on children, and the cycle of violence or trauma through generations, then our chances increase. These men are responsible for their violent and abusive behaviour. Let's educate young men and women so that violence and abuse is reduced through a better understanding of all that above.

I was talking to a young woman recently who had suffered several years of abuse without identifying it as such until she got help. She had no idea what the definition entailed and assumed that there was something wrong with her. Young women need education too, so they can recognise abuse and take action to keep themselves and their children safe.

Storytelling plays an important role in life, creating history, setting standards and expectations and illustrating behaviour. So it was in the groups. The men learned a lot from each other's stories. Their small tales of success as their emotional maturity and capacity to change their behaviour grew were invaluable. In fact, sometimes the best thing facilitators can do is not get in the way of the men.

Let's finish with a story told by one of the men.

James spoke about a time when an older man reprimanded him on a work site. James, a big man, would normally have flared up, reacting quickly with verbal abuse, taking an intimidating standover stance. This time he stopped his usual pattern and remained silent and tightly restrained. Later, when he was buying himself a coffee, he also bought one for the man, handing it to him saying, "I guess you've had a bad day. I hope this helps". The man took the coffee with surprise. Later he came and apologised to James for his behaviour.

This story so clearly illustrates how thought stopping and empathy work and how the change in one person's behaviour can change another's. The group celebrated success stories such as this.

When a facilitator left the group, the members said goodbye with these words: "Thank you for your resolute and steadfast belief that men can change their behaviour and for helping us believe and live that change."

I think this says a lot about the men themselves and what they need in order to bring about change. The "brotherhood" of the group is essential, as is the knowledge that someone standing beside them believes they can make the required changes. These men, who work hard and long to change entrenched behaviour, need to be supported and encouraged by those who believe they can do it. And while we can celebrate the changes the men made, we encourage them to share their experiences to inspire others to also make changes.

Hence this book.

CHANGE –
   A POEM

> *It is a long, long journey that never really ends*
> *But learning and growth and the benefits of friends*
> *Makes the travel worth it, for when no longer causing pain*
> *And living with that gutful of bloody guilt and shame*
> *One can reach for what is waiting on the very farthest shelf*
> *And find the greatest gift of all, the liking of oneself.*

IF ANY READER needs further information about where to go for help, please call 1800RESPECT on 1800 737 732.
   For further information, visit www.nobutsthebook.com.au

ACKNOWLEDGMENTS

My first and enormous thanks go to the many men who shared their vulnerablilies in a group setting. Twelve of them bravely wrote their story. They are the reason this book is here today. Thank you to all of those men for allowing me the privilege of working alongside them.

My friend and author Viki Wright nudged, pushed and cajoled me until I wrote a book. Her encouragement led me to compiling the men's stories in the hope that more men would seek help and more women and children would be safe. Viki got me to the starting line and I am very thankful she did.

Jodie Weber was my highly skilled proof reader, whose patience and sensitivity were greatly appreciated. Thank you so much Jodie.

Thanks to Anglicare's CEO Paul Mcdonald for giving me the go ahead in this venture. Thanks also to my then manager Jim Allen for his wisdom and advice, to Shane Bedwell for his ongoing support and assistance, to Gennene Mitchell and Bronwyn Clarkson for great supervision and support and to Kim Pedlar, Damien Litchfield, Suresh Ruberan and Shane Bedwell for being such great co-facilitators, and from whom I learnt so much.

What would I do without friends and family? Three friends in particular have been a source of wisdom and encouragement and I am very grateful to them for accepting me as-is when tired and grumpy. Love and thanks to you and to all others whose care is not forgotten.

My brother has also been of immeasurable help and will, I'm sure, be relieved when all the phone-calls and texts have finished. My big thanks to David for his measured advice and support.

Thanks also to Clinical Psychologist Bruce Falconer for his wise words have formed the preface of No Buts.

Finally, I cannot finish without acknowledging the publishing world. This has been a huge learning experience and I wish to recommend to anyone out there wanting to publish a book that you go straight to Jessica Mudditt. She will lead you, teach and support you through the publishing process. Thank you Jessica– you have been wonderful.

Nicole Webb has been an enthusiastic and skilled publicist for which I am extremely grateful and would recommend to anyone needing the right contacts in the media.

Matthew Osborne did a terrific job creating the No Buts website and I would highly recommend his work also.

Thank you all. This has been a great learning experience for me. I hope it achieves some of the outcomes we are all hoping for.